When I first heard that Larry Warner was
remember thinking that he was the right pers
personal and professional authority. Discernn
to him. It has become a way of living. I hope you'll read this book and respond to this
invitation to more fully live Jesus.

~ Alan Fadling, President and
Founder Unhurried Living and
author of *An Unhurried Life*

Larry Warner's new book distinguishes itself from all the others by its unapologetic
focus on the Holy Spirit making discernment authentically Christian. Far from the
usual notion of trying to "discover God's will" when faced with a critical decision
in life, this book underscores the fact that discernment is foremost a lifestyle we
need to cultivate. If you're looking for a theoretical or philosophical treatment on
discernment, you are bound to be disappointed; Larry's work bleeds with profuse
practicality. A great manual to own and rely upon!

~ Wil Hernandez, PhD, Obl. OSB
Executive Director, CenterQuest and
author of a trilogy on Henri Nouwen

This book is the best kind of gift: one you didn't know you wanted, but exactly what
you needed. Warner's words are deeply invitational and, by the power of the Spirit,
transformational. Between these covers you'll be introduced to saints through the
ages who have desired and pursued God's will by living Jesus and will be given
the tools to do the same. Although there are no shortcuts in Christian discernment,
I have to admit I wish I'd had this book a decade ago. The wisdom, guidance, and
encouragement within—all brought with Warner's characteristically warm style—
will be my companions in discernment for years to come.

~ Tara Owens, CSD
Spiritual Director and author of
*Embracing the Body: Finding God In
Our Flesh & Bone* and *At Play In God's
Creation: An Illuminating Coloring Book*

"The Will of God"—A phrase that brings on the proverbial "paralysis of analysis" and
leaves one insecure and doubtful or it can open a delightful door of divine adventure.
Larry Warner invites us to believe that God delights in us and does indeed have a life
for us to live. I found this book rich with insight and clearly written for the pilgrims
that want to experience the reality God intends for them.

~ Phil Strout
National Director, VineyardUSA

We have a church today because generations of Christians cultivated the practice
of honest, humble and clear discernment. But like a hard to find old-world artisan,
the Christian practices of discernment have given way to merely intellectual and
pragmatic processes. Larry Warner's *God's Will, Discernment & Living Jesus* is a

guide...back to the future. Larry is smart without being snobby; spiritual without being cliché; wise without being judgmental; and helpful without being pragmatic. Larry's book provides a mature reflection on knowing the will of God through a conversational relationship with him.

~ Todd Hunter, Anglican Bishop and
author of *Our Character at Work*

Want help in hearing and recognizing the voice of God? Read this book! Larry Warner knows that God is here and that He is inviting you into something. But: "What is God saying? To what is He calling me? And how do I know it is Him? What does the Holy Spirit sound like and how does He talk to me? What keeps me from hearing from God?" This book helps to answer those questions.

Read the work of a trustworthy, road-seasoned guide who has walked with many followers of Jesus; strong and sturdy words from a wise Ignatian-trained Spiritual Director are found here! Biblical, practical, gritty, and not always comfortable, this book will move you to prayer. Highly recommended.

~ Betsy A. Barber, PsyD
Assc. Director Institute for Spiritual
Formation, Talbot School of Theology
Director Center for Spiritual
Renewal, Biola University

In this thoughtful and winsome book, spiritual director Larry Warner, demonstrates the practical wisdom and heartfelt thinking that makes him such a trustworthy guide. Linking discernment to a "practiced way of life", Warner connects decision-making to discipleship. Offering both instructions and exercises, Warner draws from the insights of Ignatian Spirituality and his experience of spending countless hours listening to the deepest longings of people. This is a warm, deep, and profoundly helpful book. I'll be using it with my students and clients.

~ Tod Bolsinger, Vice President for
Vocation and Formation, Fuller
Seminary and author of *Canoeing
the Mountains: Christian Leadership
in Uncharted Territory.*

Imagine that Ignatius is your next door neighbor and you get to chat with him about discernment over coffee. This book is that user-friendly but also deep. It contains what we really want to know as well as a lot of things we need to know but didn't realize. Expect to be informed, enriched and delighted.

~ Jan Johnson, spiritual director and
author of *When the Soul Listens*
and *Meeting God in Scripture*

DISCERNMENT,
GOD'S WILL*&*
LIVING JESUS

Christian Discernment
as a Way of Life

LARRY WARNER

barefooted publishing

To my four grandchildren: James Patrick, Thomas Michael, Lucia Jane, and Bishop Elliot. May you each grow in your awareness of God's love for you, delight in you, and faithfulness to you—coming to know God as one who is for you, likes you, and loves loving you.

TABLE OF CONTENTS

Appendix

PREFACE

This book is a result of an unsolicited conversation God had with me. I cannot remember the exact circumstances: it was an ordinary day and I was doing ordinary things. This type of uninvited intrusion into one's everyday life often seems to be the way God makes God's will known. Anyway, I was not journaling or reading my Bible, I was not listening to worship music or an inspiring podcast. I was merely living life, and then it happened. I dare not call it a voice, but it was as clear and understandable as if someone were speaking to me.

It was not the first time I've had this type of experience, so I knew to pay attention. I knew to listen—if that's the correct word—and so I did. I "heard" God tell me to write a book on discernment. The message was unmistakable.

Let me pause for a moment and make it very clear that I am not claiming God gave me this book as you now have it. So please, if you do not like it, or if you find it offensive or badly written, you can blame me. God just told me to write it, and made no promises about whether or not it would be good!

Now, getting back to my story, I knew this was God. It was that kind of knowing where you know that you know—a knowing born out of walking with God, of living Jesus. I wish I could report that I immediately said yes and started to write, but the truth is that my response to God was, "I am not a writer." (I meant, "You've got the wrong guy.") I thought that would be the end of it, but it was not. God's response to me was short, sweet, and not all that encouraging: "I did not say you were a writer. I said to write." That was the beginning of this book.

My writing process has consisted of a series of stumbling starts and sizable stops. But God has been gracious, and I have learned much along the way. What you will find written is this book is true to my own life, the lives of those in scripture, and the lives of those I have journeyed with over the years. I do not write this book claiming to be an expert on the topic of Christian discernment. But of this I am certain: God does lead! God's will is not something that is hidden from us but something God desires that we know and walk in.

If you put the material presented in this book into practice, it will help you to become more sensitive to the communications of God, whether it is a "voice," the inner promptings of the Spirit, or some other means God uses to communicate WITH you. God has not left you alone to discern God's leading. God is the one who plays the primary role in Christian discernment. You don't have to make it happen. You have simply to be open and to follow.

May God use the material in this book to free you to live more fully into and then more fully out of the person God has created you and is calling you to be, so that you may experience more fully the wondrous life intended for you through Jesus's death, resurrection, and the subsequent gift of the indwelling, always-with-you Spirit.

INTRODUCTION

Beware! This book is dangerous. If you were hoping for a nice, safe, formulaic framework for making good decisions, a connect-the-dots, paint-by-numbers discernment process, then read no further. Christian discernment is messy, imprecise, and non-reducible, more a relationship than a recipe. You are being invited on an interactive adventure of faith that will help you become a "discerning person" rather than a "person who makes decisions." You will need to let go of certainty and control in exchange for a life of dependence, risk, faith, and trust—the kind of life Jesus lived.

Now, there is a tendency to see discernment in terms of the big decisions of life, but our focus is on Christian discernment as a relational way of life, and that takes seriously the truth that each day we are making hundreds of decisions, consciously and subconsciously —decisions that form and shape our hearts and our lives, and in turn prepare us to make the "big" decisions. This book is designed to help you to walk with God through life, open and sensitive to the leading of God.

THE PREMISES

There are two major premises that set this book apart from other books about discernment. The first is the belief that, at its core, Christian discernment is relational and flows naturally from an ongoing, real-time, interactive, conversational relationship with God. The critical foundation of this relationship is the certainty of God's love—owning and embracing the incredible-one-of-a-kind love of God—coupled with a certainty of one's identity as God's beloved.

The second major premise of this book is that the Holy Spirit plays the primary role in relational discernment. This emphatic truth is laid out in scripture and demonstrated by the life of Jesus, Paul, and others. God has not left us alone to make decisions but has given us the Spirit to guide, direct, convict, speak, and make known to us the words and thoughts of God.

THE PRACTICES

Christian Discernment as a Way of Life is a roll-up-your-sleeves manual, providing exercises/questions at the end of each chapter to help the reader develop the ability to hear and recognize the voice of Jesus, and to notice the inner promptings of the Holy Spirit. These practices are meant to be a playground on which one encounters God in freedom, openness, and honesty. The goal is that by interacting with God and self through the exercises, with a spirit of playfulness and discovery, you will gradually become more able to hear—and more willing to follow—the leading of the Spirit.

THE PRINCIPLES

In the spirit of full disclosure, I must note that many of the principles found in this book are drawn from the writings of St. Ignatius of Loyola. St. Ignatius is the recognized authority on Christian discernment and anyone who writes on that topic is forced to borrow from his writings and insights. The insights I will share with you in this book come out of over a decade's worth of time spent studying St. Ignatius' writings, teaching his wisdom to students, and putting that wisdom into practice as I journeyed alongside hundreds of individuals and helped them to recognize and follow God's leading in their lives.

THE STRUCTURE

In the first section of this book, we explore what discernment is and provide a framework for our understanding of the uniqueness of Christian discernment and the need to distinguish it from discernment in general or even from spiritual discernment. Additionally, we look at the often confusing and misunderstood phrase, *hearing God,* and bring clarity and expansion to the meaning of that phrase.

The second section of this book focuses on the person of God and the foundational love God has for each of us. It invites you to embrace your identity as God's beloved and to begin to value your relationship with God above all else. If you are not rooted and grounded in God's love and your identity as beloved, you will not be able to hear the voice of Jesus and will be hard-pressed to sense the inner promptings of the Spirit, let alone to deeply desire to follow as God leads you. This relational component is the soil from which your ability to recognize the communications of God must grow; it is what will allow you to distinguish good from evil, perceive what is best and embody God's will.

The third section presents the biblical foundations upon which everything is built. It looks at what constitutes the will of God while also exploring the indispensable role the Holy Spirit and scripture play in leading the people of God.

In the fourth section you will explore three modes of decision-making: the pyrotechnics of God, the inner promptings of God, and pros and cons. Additionally, you will be invited to explore the use of your imagination as a helpful tool when making a decision. Now, although you may feel tempted to immediately turn to this section, please resist the temptation to do so. The ability to use any of these modes in a helpful, God-honoring way is contingent upon developing a relational life with God and understanding the role the Holy Spirit and scripture play in Christian discernment. In other words, the information outlined in the first three sections of this book is indispensable to understanding the tools of the fourth section.

I need to make a decision NOW!

The premise of this book is that Christian discernment is a way of life that is relational in nature. However, if you picked up this book because you have a big decision to make and are looking for help, then I would encourage you to read Section Four. I do hope you'll read the entire book at some point so that you may develop a discerning way of life. This is important because we make decisions every day that mold and shape who we are. Finally, let me encourage you to truly consider whether the decision you feel you have to make immediately is one that you actually do need to make immediately—though it may feel horribly urgent, it might not be as pressing as it appears. However, if it is, then the first thing you might want to do is to ask for additional time to decide. All they can say is no.

The fifth section is intended to help you cultivate the abilities needed to order your life in such a way that you are more open and sensitive to God's communication and the inner movements of the Spirit. Important insights regarding discernment along with interactive practices provide the reader an expanding and deepening opportunity to live relationally with Jesus.

A distinctive feature of this fifth section is that the chapters are not designed to be read in any particular order; rather the reader or group going through this material is encouraged to prayerfully discern which chapter is most inviting, suitable, or timely to begin next. This unstructured approach provides an opportunity to listen for and pay attention to the communications of God and the inner promptings of the Spirit as you make your way through this entire section.

Alone or Together

Although this book can and will be read individually, I believe it would be more beneficial to process your insights and discoveries in the context of a group. Going through the material with others fosters positive accountability around the practices, provides opportunity for deeper discussion, and embraces and celebrates the uniqueness of each person's experience with God.

THE WEBSITE

Additional exercises, materials for leading small groups, and short videos for each chapter can be found at www.b-ing.org under *Christian Discernment*. These are all free and the materials are for you to use as you see fit.

FINAL THOUGHTS

If you believe Jesus is alive and that real-time encounters with God are possible, even expected; if you feel God is calling you to become a person of discernment, rather than one who simply makes decisions; if you desire to live a Jesus-focused life, sensitive to the promptings and invitations of the Holy Spirit, this book is for you. Let the adventure begin.

SECTION ONE: FIRST THINGS FIRST

In this section we will explore what we mean by the term Christian discernment as well as the phrase hearing God. As you make your way through this section, and the rest of the book, pay attention to those things you are drawn to and resistant toward. Begin to see resistance as an invitation to turn aside and pay attention, to reflect on and then respond to what you discover. This recognizing, reflecting on, and responding to are key components in the process of Christian discernment, so as you recognize and pay attention to what you are drawn to and resistant toward, you are training yourself to become a discerning person.

CHAPTER ONE

THE WHAT AND WHY OF DISCERNMENT

This book is an invitation into a life with God. Rather than offering a method or process by which discernment is acquired, I am advocating a way of being that cultivates the capacity already within us to hear and follow Jesus.

But I'm getting ahead of myself. Before getting into the cultivation and nurturing of Christian discernment, it is important to step back and explore the meaning of discernment, as well as the presuppositions that underlie the truths presented in the chapters ahead. Let's start with some basic questions:

- What is discernment?
- What is spiritual discernment and how does it differ from "intellectual" discernment?
- What is Christian discernment, and why is it important to differentiate it as Christian? Why not simply spiritual?
- What is the relationship of discernment to decision-making?

There are questions sprinkled throughout this chapter, as well as at the end, to help you explore these issues for yourself, and to launch into a conversation with others. If your group is interested in discussing the topic, these questions can help you express your thoughts and appreciate the thoughts of others, as you make this journey together.

WHAT IS DISCERNMENT?

Discernment refers to the act of using one's mental ability and/or senses to recognize something as being different or distinct; to separate, to differentiate.

HOW DOES SPIRITUAL DISCERNMENT DIFFER FROM INTELLECTUAL DISCERNMENT?

Spiritual discernment is quite different than discernment that relies solely on the abilities of the mind and senses. This type of discernment points to a reality beyond what one can see, touch, taste, or even think. Spiritual discernment moves us away from the concrete into something or someone that transcends the finite framework of time and space; it shifts our focus beyond the known material world to a supernatural source of wisdom and existence. The process employed here is more sensing than thinking, more felt than reasoned.

HOW DOES CHRISTIAN DISCERNMENT DIFFER FROM SPIRITUAL DISCERNMENT?

Let me begin by saying that most who write on this topic don't differentiate between spiritual discernment and Christian discernment. But for the purposes of this book, I believe it's necessary to highlight the specific realities of Christian discernment that are not inferred when the term *spiritual discernment* is used.

Christian discernment is a by-product of Jesus' life, death, and resurrection combined with the imparting of the Holy Spirit to all who believe. It is the Holy Spirit that implants the capacity to hear and understand the words and thoughts of God (1 Cor. 2:10–15) for we now have the mind of Christ (1 Cor. 2:16).

Christian discernment is made possible through the Holy Spirit and it, like spiritual discernment, surpasses the categories of the ordinary, embracing the transcendent mystery of eternity, of God and of God's wisdom made available to us through the Spirit. Our ability to discern is no longer limited to our own mind, senses, or common sense, for we have the Spirit to guide us and make the communications of God known to us. So, although there are definite similarities between spiritual discernment and Christian discernment, they are also very different.

SO WHAT IS CHRISTIAN DISCERNMENT?

Christian discernment is the ability within us—energized and empowered by the Spirit—to: 1) recognize the communications of God in expected and unexpected places, 2) distinguish good from evil, 3) perceive what is best, and, 4) embody God's will. Christian discernment is not something we are able to manufacture. It is an ability made possible by the indwelling of the Holy Spirit.

As Christians, we have the Spirit-empowered ability to *recognize the communications of God,* and this raises two important questions: 1) what is God communicating, and, 2) how do I know it is God who is communicating it? It is through the Spirit, combined with our experiential learning of listening to God, that we expand our capability to hear and recognize God's communications to us, in whatever form they may take—to be certain it's not the voice of an imposter or even our own wishful thinking. As John tells us in John 10:4–5, "…and the sheep follow him, for they *know his voice.* A stranger they will not follow, but they will flee from him, for they do not know the voice of strangers" (emphasis mine). One aim of this book is to help you to become more aware of, more in tune with, the communications of God.

The mere possessing of the ability for Christian discernment does not guarantee a capability to even distinguish good from evil, as the writer of Hebrews reminds us, "…for the mature, for those who have their powers of discernment trained by constant practice to distinguish good from evil" (5:14b). Though God is the primary actor, we have a part to play in the cultivation of Christian discernment.

The gifts of the Spirit

Christian discernment is something every Christian has the ability to develop and is not the same as the specific gift referred to as "the ability to distinguish between spirits" in 1 Cor. 12:10. The distinguishing between spirits involves the ability to intuitively recognize and distinguish between the influence of God, Satan, the world, and the flesh in a given situation. Christian discernment also has an aspect of the discernment of spirits but unlike the spiritual gift mentioned above, which is a supernatural ability bestowed by the Holy Spirit, this is a skill developed over time with practice and making use of the insights given in Chapter 12.

As one develops the ability to *distinguish good from evil*—an indication of spiritual maturity and growth—Satan begins to change his strategy. He begins to employ subtlety and subterfuge—taking on the appearance of an angel of light—and even uses initially good things to get us off track or to keep us from the best. Christian discernment, which is always important, becomes even more important when you consider the changing strategy of Satan. For the world is not black and white, and things are not always what they appear to be. Since Satan will even use good for his own ends (more on this in chapter 12), the need to *perceive what is best* (as opposed to what is merely good) becomes extremely important.

Finally, *embodying God's will* is the fourth expression of the ability to discern, and it is energized and empowered by the Spirit. *Embodying God's will* refers to living out God's will from the heart, as opposed to mere performance of God's will. Embodying God's will becomes possible as we are able to distinguish good from evil, perceive the best, and recognize the communications of God.

> *The will of God becomes something we are, rather than something we do.*

Cultivating and Nurturing Christian Discernment

It is important to remember that we do not manufacture Christian discernment through our own efforts but are expected to cultivate that which the Spirit has energized and empowered within us. This continuing cultivation of Christian discernment is nurtured by a practiced way of life involving: 1) a deepening knowledge of God and self, 2) uniquely living Jesus, 3) attending and responding to the Holy Spirit, and, 4) desiring God's greater glory.

Before unpacking these four components that cultivate and nurture Christian discernment, let's explore the phrase, *practiced way of life*. This phrase stresses that you have a part to play. The writer of Hebrews makes this point when he admonishes his readers for their inability to discern between good and evil, *because* of their failure to train themselves (Heb. 5:12–14). The passage makes it clear that the development of Christian discernment is not automatic; the individual has an active role in the process. It is your responsibility to cultivate and nurture this Spirit-endowed ability through a practiced way of life. And that's exactly what this book is intended to help you do.

This *practiced way of life* is characterized by four things:

1. *A deepening knowledge of God and self.* Your faith is established and grown through a deepening knowledge of God and self. Nearly 500 years ago, John Calvin, an early reformer of the Church, penned these words: "Our wisdom, insofar as it ought to be deemed true and solid wisdom, consists almost entirely of two parts: the knowledge of God and of ourselves."[1]

   Your image of God and your image of self are of paramount importance when it comes to developing a way of life that cultivates and nurtures Christian discernment. For example, if you view God as judgmental, punitive, and vengeful—that is, in a negative light—then you will not desire to trust God, to follow God's leading, and certainly not to surrender your will to God. If you see yourself as unloved by God, unworthy, and needing to earn God's love, you will consequently be hindered in your ability to sense God's presence and leading in your life.

The degree to which you are able to embrace and internalize the knowledge of who God is (as one who is for you and not against you) and who you are (a new creation, fully and unconditionally loved by God) will be the degree to which you are willing to listen to and follow the voice of Jesus. At its core, Christian discernment is about a relationship—God's relationship with you and your relationship with God. This is why chapters 3 and 4 focus on *whose* we are (exploring the person of God) and *who* we are (exploring the truth of who you are in Christ).

2. *Uniquely living Jesus.* This rather daunting expression refers to ordering your life in harmony with the words and teachings of Jesus in a way that is consistent with the person God has created and called you to be.

   The phrase "live Jesus" was coined in the 1600's and is reminiscent of Galatians 2:20 where Paul writes, "I have been crucified with Christ. It is no longer I who live, but Christ who lives in me. And the life I now live in the flesh I live by faith in the Son of God, who loved me and gave himself for me."

   For me, the phrase *living Jesus* is shorthand for a life lived and ordered in harmony with the life-transforming realities that flow to us from the death and resurrection of Jesus and the indwelling of the Spirit. It speaks of living life out of an awareness of who one is in Christ as a new creation—forgiven, justified, sanctified, adopted, beloved...now able to live a God-honoring life, partnering with what God is doing in and through us. *Living Jesus* is a life of dependence on the power of Christ, the leading of the Spirit, and the knowledge that one is loved by God, desiring above all that God's kingdom come and God's will be done on earth as it is in heaven.

3. *Attending and responding to the Holy Spirit.* This twofold ability is developed by practice. The exercises in this book are designed to help you grow in your awareness of the inner movements and promptings of the Spirit as you walk day-by-day through life. Jesus has not left us alone, but has given us the Spirit to lead and guide us. Our responsibility is to learn to sense this leading and guiding, which begins with developing awareness.

4. *Desiring God's greater glory.* As it was with Jesus, the primary motivation shaping our discernment is the desire to glorify God. It is this internal perspective that fosters the ability to deny oneself and say with Jesus "not my will but God's will be done." This desire for God's greater glory and the willingness to seek God's glory above one's own glory, comfort, and security, can only flow from a deep knowledge of God and self. And so we're back where we started, full circle through the four interrelated components of the practiced way of life!

Exercise:

Which one of the four components listed above do you feel is easiest for you? Which is the most challenging to you? Please remember that this is about awareness, not condemnation—be honest.

As you gradually internalize the four components above, your capacity to practice Christian discernment will broaden and deepen. You will be more confident in your ability to distinguish good from evil, to recognize the voice of Jesus and to embody God's will as a way of life. Be patient with yourself—this process is a lifelong journey. But being on this journey will produce a greater freedom to live into and out of the person God created you to be, and to experience in more meaningful ways God's presence with you, God's delight in you, God's love for you, and God's faithfulness to you.

WHY IS CHRISTIAN DISCERNMENT IMPORTANT?

Now, having distinguished between discernment, spiritual discernment, and Christian discernment, as well as having examined some aspects of the components of Christian discernment and the importance of cultivating it, let's explore why Christian discernment is so important. This partial list of Biblical passage summaries points to the critical need to develop and nurture Christian discernment in our lives:

- God's thoughts and God's ways are not our thoughts/ways. (Isa. 55:8–9)

- Wolves appear in sheep's clothing. (Matt. 7:15)

- Satan appears as an angel of light. (2 Cor. 11:14)

- We do not believe every spirit, but test the spirits to see whether they are from God. (1 John 4:1)

- We are in a spiritual battle. (Eph. 6:10–12)

- The world and the Christian life are in opposition. (James 4:4)

- God's wisdom can seem like foolishness. (1 Cor. 1:25)

- We can grieve the Holy Spirit. (Eph. 4:30)

- We have to be careful how we walk…we are not to be foolish, but are to understand the will of the Lord. (Eph. 5:15–17)

Even a quick perusal of these few passages demonstrates the necessity of Christian discernment. They make it clear that evil is not always easily distinguished from good, that God's ways and God's wisdom can appear foreign and even foolish, that we are in a spiritual battle and that it is possible to grieve the Holy Spirit. In this world, where the devil can parade as an angel of light, Christian discernment is not a nice extra, a talent to pull out in a pinch; it is absolutely necessary to live Jesus.

> Exercise:
>
> *From the nine reasons listed above what would you say are the top three reasons for the continuing cultivation of Christian discernment? Why?*

THE PRESUPPOSITIONS

Finally, spend some time exploring the presuppositions listed below, for they convey the foundational beliefs for the material found in this book. As you slowly read through the list below, ask yourself the following questions:

Which one(s) do you agree with? Which one(s) are you resistant toward, not comfortable with, not so sure of? Which would you rank as your top three? Which would you rank as your bottom three? Why?

- God is active in the world, in you, and through your life.
- God knows you, loves you, is for you, and is powerful and wise.
- Real-time encounters with the Risen Christ are possible.
- God speaks to you.
- The Holy Spirit is an active and ongoing guide in discernment.
- God leads you uniquely, individually, and particularly.
- You play an important role in discernment.
- Christian discernment is a byproduct of ongoing and deepening relationship with God.
- The scriptures play a critical role in your embodying God's will.
- Christian discernment is linked to a deep desire that God's kingdom come and God's will be done.
- Christian discernment involves an integration of the heart and mind.
- Your image of God and knowledge of self are the critical components impacting the ability to discern.
- God has an individual will for your life, which may often be broad like a meadow or, at times, specific like a bullseye.
- You can grow and are expected to grow in your ability to discern as a result of practice and experience.

DECISION-MAKING AND CHRISTIAN DISCERNMENT

Sadly, over the last few centuries, decision-making has become separated from Christian discernment. Instead of decision-making being viewed as an outflow of a way of life with Jesus, decisions large and small are consistently made without reference to God, by listing pros and cons or by using common sense. This is true even of Christians! "Discernment" has become an intellectual exercise, a practical atheism that tacitly disavows the leading of the Spirit and embraces pragmatically-inspired means of making decisions. When decision-making sidesteps reliance on the Spirit and the need for a discerning way of life, individuals opens themselves up to a myriad of dangers and difficulties.

This is not to say that there is no place for rules and insights related to making decisions (see Section Four), but the emphasis needs to be on living a life that cultivates sensitivity to the Spirit and is receptive to the communications of God, so that your heart is ordered to desire God's greater glory and the embodiment of God's will above all else.

Good decision-making grows out of the soil of a practiced way of life.

EXERCISES:

1. I define Christian discernment as the ability within us, energized and empowered by the Spirit, to: 1) recognize the communications of God, 2) distinguish good from evil, 3) perceive what is best, and, 4) embody God's will. Christian discernment is not something we are able to manufacture. It is an ability made possible by the indwelling of the Holy Spirit.

Which component would you characterize as your greatest strength? Which is the area where you have the greatest potential for improvement? Why? Are there any components of this definition that you are not comfortable with? Why?

2. Think about the possibility of living a life in which you walk with Jesus, hear Jesus' voice, sense the prompting of the Spirit, and embody God's will. What feelings arise as you imagine such intimacy with God? What fears and concerns, if any, surface? Do you actually believe it is possible? Why or why not?

Can you think of a time in your life when this was a reality? What was it like? What has changed?

CHAPTER TWO
HEARING GOD

G od, are you talking to me?

Christian discernment is relational at its core, and this God-initiated relationship presupposes that God is involved in our lives—God who is with us, within us, communicating to us, guiding and directing us. God has not left us alone with the Bible to figure out how to live, but has given the Holy Spirit to help us know God's words and thoughts, so that we are personally led by the God of all creation.

God is a God who communicates. In the beginning God spoke, and God has never stopped speaking. In Jesus, God brought us back into a deep and personal relationship: we are now friends of God, children of God, the beloved of God, the very abiding place of God. Jesus tells us that he calls us by name and that we will know his voice and follow him (John 10:3-4). Jesus assures us that he will give us the Holy Spirit, who will make his words and teachings known to us (John 14:26,16:13), and Paul states that we will be led by the Spirit (Rom. 8:14), who will make the words and thoughts of God known to us (1 Cor. 2:15).

God is committed to the ongoing process of communication and it is the

Spirit that empowers us to enjoy a continual open channel of communication with God. We will explore three aspects of this divine conversation below:

1. What does it mean that God speaks?

2. Why do I sometimes find it difficult to hear from God?

3. How do I know God is communicating with me?

WHAT DOES IT MEAN THAT GOD SPEAKS?

When we speak about hearing from God or mention following the voice of Jesus, it can be a source of pain or frustration for some. Many, while believing God speaks and leads, don't recognize this experience in their own lives. Often this is a result of a limited view of what is meant by hearing from God. This point was driven home to me at a weekend retreat I recently led.

I began our final session asking the group, "What have you heard from God during our time together this weekend?" Immediately a person in the group started to cry. This same woman had shared the first night that she knew God had wanted her to attend the retreat; each time we gathered as a group she was engaged and willing to share. But now, as she confessed she had not heard God speak this weekend or ever, she was sobbing. It was obvious from her earlier sharing that God had communicated to her in significant ways during our time together. I walked her through the weekend, reflecting to her what she had shared the first night and during our group times. As I spoke, her crying began to subside, and then suddenly she was crying again—realizing that God had communicated to her not only this weekend, but throughout her life.

God showed me through this encounter that when we speak of God's voice, the immediate thought of many is that it must be audible. And since many, even most, have not heard an audible voice, they assume that God is not speaking. But this is not the case. As the woman at the retreat realized, hearing from God can mean much more than hearing words spoken out loud. My prayer for you is that your understanding of how God communicates will be expanded and, like the woman at the retreat, that you'll discover that God has been speaking and is speaking to you.

BEGIN AT THE BEGINNING

God speaks! Immediately in Genesis, we see that God speaks and that God's words are powerful—God speaks creation itself into existence! As soon as God creates Adam and Eve, God engages in conversation with them, and so it goes. God continues to communicate with Noah, Abraham, Sarah, Joseph, Moses, David, Isaiah, Mary, Peter, Paul, John...the list goes on and on.

And it doesn't stop at the spoken word. God uses burning bushes, visions, a donkey, angels, dreams, prophets, Moses' father-in-law, a still small voice, creation, the person of Jesus, the gift of the Holy Spirit and the Bible to communicate to those who have ears to hear. The scriptures make two things crystal clear: 1) God communicates, and, 2) God uses a variety of creative communication forms.

Exercise:

Take some time to explore your own experience and ask yourself how God has spoken. Think back—ask God to help you recall the times you felt or "heard" from God and what form that took. Next turn to the worksheet at the end of this chapter for a list of the various ways God communicates. Consider with an open mind which ones you find comfortable and why; which are more challenging and why? I hope this exercise will help you to become more aware of the ways God has and is communicating to you, while also expanding your awareness of the variety of ways God communicates, so you are better equipped to recognize the expected and unexpected communications of God.

THE HOLY SPIRIT: GAME-CHANGER

As followers of Christ, we have the ultimate game-changer within us. In the Holy Spirit, given freely to all believers, we possess a greater consciousness, and an enhanced capacity to hear God's words and discern God's will. As a consequence of the Spirit within us, we are privy to the words and thoughts of God (1 Cor. 2:15) and we have the mind of Christ (1 Cor. 2:16). We can freely hear from God, recognize the communications of God, and even understand God's Spirit.

Sometimes the Spirit communicates in whispers, "the still small voice" or the "inner voice", a quiet presence within us that uses our own thoughts, impressions, feelings, and sensitivities —Spirit to spirit—to guide us and direct us. This form of communication seems to be generated from within but can be just as clear as an external audible voice. Since Christ lives within us and Christ IS our life, and "it is no longer I who live, but Christ who lives in me" (Gal. 2:20), it makes sense that God would work through our own thoughts, impressions, feelings, and sensitivities to communicate with us.

I believe these inner promptings of the Spirit are the most prevalent way God communicates with us. This form of communication often goes beyond words and involves a deep knowing that is difficult to explain, but when experienced and trusted, is easily recognized. St. Ignatius, writing about this inner awareness, likens it to a drop of water gently landing on a sponge or a drop of water hitting a rock. When we are moving from good to better, it is like a drop of water gently landing on a sponge. When we are moving away from the good, it feels like a drop of water hitting a rock. In the first case, the drop of water gently landing on a sponge, there is a deep inner sense that *this is right, this is good*—a deep knowing that this is the proper path. Whereas a drop of water hitting a rock speaks of inner discord, a knowing or sense that *this is not right*. Both are subtle feelings, and it takes time to cultivate a sensitivity to them, but once cultivated, that sensitivity can be trusted and depended on.

Exercise:

To illustrate the subtleness of what I am talking about, but also the clarity a subtle feeling can bring, fold your hands, interlacing your fingers. Then simply switch the positions of your thumbs and pay attention to how that feels. It will not be a significant difference, but noticeable. One way feels correct and the other feels incorrect. Spend a moment here to reflect; this is the same subtle feeling of the drop-of-water example mentioned above. The next section of the book is intended to help you cultivate and nourish the ability to become more sensitive to this inner prompting of the Spirit.

HOW ELSE DOES GOD SPEAK?

God also communicates, in conjunction with the Holy Spirit, through the scriptures. The God-given scriptures contain helpful teaching for living a God-honoring life, a life consistent with the person whom God has called you and created you to be. However, when we read the scriptures, we need to allow the Spirit to speak to us through them, allowing the Spirit to guide and direct our time in God's word. God speaks powerfully and clearly through the Bible. In Section Three, we will spend time unpacking the critically important role the Spirit and scripture play in Christian discernment.

WHY DO I SOMETIMES FIND IT DIFFICULT TO HEAR FROM GOD?

If God is committed to ongoing communication with us, why do so many fail to hear God speak? Below are a number of reasons people do not hear God. In my life, one of the reasons is that at times I do not *want* to hear from God. I want to do what I want to do. What about you? Please read through the list below prayerfully. After you finish reading, you will be invited to choose which reasons are currently true in your own life.

1. I find it difficult to hear God because I have a limited view of what "hearing God" means.

2. I don't trust myself when it comes to hearing from God or determining if it was God doing the communicating, so I quickly dismiss the possibility that God was actually speaking to me.

3. I do not want to hear from God. I want to do what I want, when I want, and the way I want. I want to be in control.

4. I have too much noise, internal and external, in my life to be able to hear God.

5. Because I am always in a hurry, always on the go, I can't be present to the One who is present to me, present within me, and in whose presence I live, move, and have my being. I do not have space in my life to hear from God.

6. I do not expect God to speak to me.

7. I have not developed a conversational relationship with God because I doubt God will speak to me.

8. I have not spent time cultivating and nourishing sensitivity to the Spirit so that I am able to recognize that subtle prompting, a drop of water hitting a sponge or rock.

9. I have not taken the time to become familiar with the voice of Jesus or with the ways God communicates with me, so it is difficult for me to distinguish God's voice amidst the cacophony of other voices in the world.

Choose two or three of the above which, at this point in your life, are true for you. And please remember this is not about condemnation, but awareness—"there is therefore now no condemnation for those who are in Christ Jesus" (Rom. 8:1). Once you make your choices from the list, take some time to explore why these choices are true of your life.

And take heart! The exercises, practices, and reflection questions in the chapters ahead are designed to heighten your awareness and to help you become more able to recognize God's voice, whatever form it may take, and then to follow those promptings. Trust God and trust the process. We are just getting started.

HOW DO I KNOW IT IS GOD COMMUNICATING WITH ME?

The simple answer to this question is: by experience. Just as a baby learns to recognize the voice of her mommy and daddy, a deepening relationship with God will help us learn to recognize the communications of God and become more in tune with the inner promptings of the Spirit. We will learn the cadence of God's voice, the tone, the unique characteristics with which God speaks to us—we will be able to recognize God's communication amidst all the other competing voices, both within and without.

Imagine two friends walking into a crowded indoor mall. People are scurrying here and there like ants on an anthill, yet one of the two friends suddenly stops and says to the other, "Do you hear that? There is a cricket in here," and he walks over to a nearby planter and pulls out a cricket. His companion can't believe it and asks how, in the midst of all this commotion, could he hear the sound of a cricket? The friend gently put the cricket back and then says, "Watch this." He then reaches into his pocket, pulls out a few coins and drops them on the floor. Suddenly, almost everyone around them stops in their tracks and turns their attention toward the clanging coins, for they all knew the sound of coins hitting the floor.

I like this story because it makes a number of points. As busy people in a noisy and often frenetic world, we have been trained to listen for and to certain things, while remaining oblivious to others. It is not surprising that Jesus' prayer was for those who have ears to hear, because just having ears does not guarantee that we will hear God when God communicates to us.

GETTING STARTED

Perhaps now is the time for you to begin to be open to the possibility that God is speaking to you and to lean into the messages you are hearing from God. I'm not inviting you to follow with abandon, but to follow slowly, as if you were seeking to determine whether or not a frozen lake was safe to walk on. Ask God to open you to promptings of the Spirit, to open your ears to the communications of God—whatever form they may take.

As you begin to hear from God, ask yourself, "Is what I am hearing or coming to understand in harmony with the scriptures and character of God? Am I aware of the inner leading of the Spirit? Is it a drop of water gently landing on a sponge or hitting a rock?" If it feels like water hitting a rock, don't even begin to follow what you heard. But if you sense a *yes*, a drop of water gently landing on a sponge, and it is consistent with scripture and the person of Jesus, then gently and attentively move forward, continuing to listen, continuing to be internally aware.

As stated earlier, many people respond with distrust when something within stirs, believing it couldn't possibly be from God, and they dismiss it. We are going to work to change that distrust, since there is nothing more natural nor more to be expected than that God is a God who loves to communicate to God's children. Let's begin to live into that truth!

Finally, in addition to living life with a Godward ear, I also invite you to ask God to guide and direct you in the everyday coming and goings of your life. I am not implying that God deeply cares about every single detail of your life—what to wear, where to sit—as there is much freedom in Christ, but I am inviting you to just ask. Ask God when you go to church where God may want you to sit, ask what line to get in at the store, which way to drive home, is there anyone God wants you to call, text, write to, visit. Jesus, speaking of himself, says that he did "nothing of [my] own accord" (John 5:19). Jesus is not inferring that God is a micromanager, but Jesus IS communicating an inner desire and predisposition to listen for and to the voice of God and the leading of the Spirit. I do not think God, for the most part, cares where we sit in church, but by asking we are opening ourselves up to the truth that God does guide and direct us and may actually do so.

I was teaching an eight-week class on discernment and invited those attending to ask God each week where they were to sit in church. Only one out of the seven times did I sense God directing me to a place other than where I would normally sit. That time I ended up celebrating communion next to a favorite elder lady in the church and exchanging a hug with her afterwards. That was my final memory of this wonderful saint, because she died the following day. I am not inferring that a similar experience will happen to you because you ask God to lead and direct, but I know that when I live that way, that type of thing tends to occur more often.

MOVING FORWARD

As we come to the end of Section One, you have a choice in front of you: you either proceed to Section Two of this book, or to Section Three. Section Two firmly grounds you in relationship with God, the soil out of which your life of discernment will grow. I placed it next because I feel it's important to begin practicing the exercises in this section sooner rather than later. However, some readers may feel more comfortable beginning with Section Three, which focuses on the critical role of scripture and the Holy Spirit in Christian discernment, while also examining what is and what is not God's will. Skipping ahead to Section Three will work too.

Now it's your choice—and it's your chance to practice Christian discernment. Listen for the communications of God and the promptings of the Spirit regarding what to read next: Section Two or Section Three. Don't agonize, because, as with many of the decisions we face daily, there is really no wrong choice. It's essentially the same as "paper or plastic?" But by asking the question, you are inviting God to be a part of your journey and learning to recognize the ways God communicates to you.

EXERCISES:

1. Do you believe God still speaks to people, leads people, shares God's plans with people, calls people by name, walks before us, and beckons us to follow OR has God abandoned us when it comes to decision-making? Are we left to fend for ourselves, making use of scripture, common sense, and conventional wisdom to make the best decisions we can, or can we walk with Jesus, be led by Jesus, and hear from the Triune God? Why or Why not?

2. How does God speak to you? (See table on the next page.)

   a. First column of blanks: Indicate which ways God has communicated to you.

   b. Second column: Choose the five most trustworthy ways God communicates and then rank them in terms of importance (1=highest, 5=lowest)

   c. Third column: Choose the 3 most undependable ways to rely on if one wants to hear from God.

DAILY PRACTICE:

Each day, go back through your day asking God to show you those times God was seeking to speak to you, to lead you. When did you hear and follow? When did you hear and not follow? When did you not hear? When did you not want to hear from God? Then explore the "why's" behind your answers.

Bible _____ _____ _____

Reason _____ _____ _____

Circumstances _____ _____ _____

Common Sense _____ _____ _____

Feelings/emotions _____ _____ _____

Audibly _____ _____ _____

Internal voice of God _____ _____ _____

External voice of God _____ _____ _____

Your Body _____ _____ _____

Community _____ _____ _____

Special Revelation _____ _____ _____

Wise Counsel _____ _____ _____

Dreams _____ _____ _____

Desires _____ _____ _____

Visions _____ _____ _____

Creation _____ _____ _____

"Mouth of babes" and others _____ _____ _____

Inner promptings of the Spirit _____ _____ _____

Inner sense of knowing _____ _____ _____

Silence _____ _____ _____

SECTION TWO: DEVELOPING A WAY OF LIFE—LIVING JESUS

This section presents the knowings, attitudes, and key practices that will help you begin to live Jesus—that is, to live a life knowing who God is and who you are, while being attentive to the Spirit and able to say not my will but God's will be done. In the upcoming pages, you will be exposed to the truths that can begin to transform you from a person who makes decisions into a discerning person who embodies God's will. This is a very important section: the ability to live into and out of the truths and insights regarding discernment and decision-making (presented later, in Section Four) will be possible only to the degree you have been able to internalize and embrace what you will read, ponder, and reflect on here in Section Two.

Chapter Three

Whose Are You?

The Orientation-Disorientation-Reorientation of Knowing God

The bus was speeding downhill, going too fast to make the next turn. I was seated to the right of the bus driver, the first seat by the door. The bus was filled with high school students returning from winter camp. I slid to the edge of my seat and asked the bus driver if something was wrong. He told me we had no brakes. The bus continued to pick up speed. I stood up, turned to the students, and told them to grab pillows, jackets—anything soft—and cover their heads, and I would then tell them what to do next.

The next thing I remember is helicopters landing. The bus was on its side, much further down the hill than I was. We were airlifted to five different hospitals. Two riders lost their lives, one of whom I had baptized just the week prior. She had been sitting on the seat across from me.

This fatal accident led all of us to question God's identity and character. We left camp that morning knowing God loved us and was faithful to us. We asked specifically for traveling mercies, and now this! As we had boarded the bus that morning, each of us had an internalized sense of God cultivated over time, an amalgamation of what we had heard, read, and experienced. It may or may not have been theologically accurate, but it worked for us. It helped us to make sense of life until it didn't. On that Sunday our current image of God, our God orientation, was shattered.

When our orientation (what we have come to know and believe) becomes disorientation (what we know and believe is called into question), we have choices to make. Am I going to enter into and walk through this time of disorientation with God, give up on God altogether, or just pretend that nothing has changed and do my best to maintain the beliefs about God I held before all this happened—an image incongruent with reality but one that brings some level of comfort? The pathway of growth is through the disorientation, but it is a painful path: confusing, maddening, and often quite lonely. We were fortunate in that there were dozens of us together on this path, each individually wrestling with the question: How did a loving God allow this to happen to God's children?

Without letting God off the hook, we come to God with our raw, unedited feelings and questions. In disorientation, we become profoundly and painfully aware that the old, the comfortable, and the known is gone, and that the new has not yet come. However, in time, the new knowing, the new awareness begins to form and take shape and we slowly enter into reorientation. This is precisely how our image of God is exposed and expanded. It's an ongoing process that we are invited into again and again and again. One day our God orientation makes sense. Then not...a move, a divorce, loss of a child, job, house, a provocative book, internal angst, *this is not working anymore*...it all no longer rings true. We begin to realize that our image of God is woefully inadequate; it's like returning to one's elementary school and finding that it seems suddenly smaller, rundown, not really useful. The critical question for each of us is: will I stay the course, seeking to trust God and the process, willing to pray, "I believe; help me in my unbelief"? If we are able to remain on the journey, a new insight into the character of God will form; we will reach a level of comfort-ability with this new God-identity and enter into a time of reorientation. We learn to live life in light of this new God-image until the cycle begins again. We discover that God is like the horizon: each time it seems to be getting closer, it expands.

Today I believe, as I always have, that God is loving, powerful, wise, and faithful. But the meaning of those words for me has radically changed. I trust God far more today than ever before, but I no longer trust God to do what I want or even what makes sense to me. I trust God to be God: one who is loving, powerful, wise, faithful, full of grace and mercy—I trust in the person and character of God, the message of the cross and the empty tomb. How that will look in my own life or the lives of those I love, I can't know. But I know in whom I believe, and God is faithful.

LET ME TAKE A MOMENT TO DEFINE
ORIENTATION-DISORIENTATION-REORIENTATION

Orientation is a place comfort and security with God. We know what we know and it is working for us in the current reality of our life. The temptation is to never want to leave this place even when the comfort and security appear to be more illusion than reality. There were many in the church I attended who never really wrestled with God over what happened, choosing to find refuge in what they currently knew to be true—an opportunity lost.

Disorientation involves a growing realization, sometimes sudden, that what you thought you knew you are no longer so sure about and are beginning to question. The practices and truths that once worked well in your relationship with God are no longer helpful—something is shifting and you can begin to feel the comfort and security of orientation ebbing away. This is often a lonely time that is only understood by those who have been on this part of the journey before—others will feel threatened, and might even doubt your faith. It is good to have another person with you as you journey through the shadow of death that is disorientation. It is important to be patient with yourself, endeavoring to trust God and the process, resisting the temptation to run back to orientation.

Reorientation is a welcome oasis after a period of disorientation. It is a time to try to live into and out of what you have unlearned and learned during disorientation. You now see, hear, and experience things differently—God, yourself, theology, the Church—but eventually you become settled, comfortable with questions and ambiguity, and once again you begin to experience a level of security and comfort—not based on the certainty of *what* you know but on *who* you have come to know and experience in a deeper way. This eventually becomes a new orientation that will lead to a new disorientation for, since God is infinite, our image of God will continue to be expanding and deepening.

Now if you are serious about expanding and deepening your experiential knowing of God, you don't need to create a crisis in your life. Crisis will come—it could be through encounters with a friend or foe as they question your beliefs, a book you read that challenges the assumptions of your faith, attending a different type of church, or through the circumstances that are a result of living in a broken world where evil, injustice and death are daily realities of life. Whatever the source, when you encounter crisis the choice is yours. You can choose to trust God and the process, choosing to enter into times of disorder without seeking to control, or you can suppress your feelings/questions, or spiritualize them away. If you choose to embrace this new challenge, I encourage you to seek a spiritual director or a spiritual mentor—someone who has experienced and journeyed through a season of disorientation with God and is able to be with you in it. They are not to rescue you but to create a hospitable presence, to listen deeply, to give grace and encouragement, to provide space for you to openly, honestly, and freely process without judgment.

Discernment as a way of life presupposes a level of maturity that is a by-product of one's image of God, so it's important to take time to explore, to become aware of, and hopefully to expand your image of who God is. Jesus states that eternal life involves knowing God; Jeremiah says knowing and understanding who God is, is to be valued above wisdom, power or riches;

Paul prays that those who already know Jesus would continue to grow in their knowledge of God. Your knowledge of God—that is, your internalized belief about who God is—forms and shapes how you live your life, the choices you make.

When you have a narrow, fixed view of God, you naturally deny realities that are contrary to that view or spiritualize those things in your life that would threaten your static image of God. This is done by "letting God off the hook" for the unacceptable, pain filled realities of life, or by spiritualizing circumstances that challenge your preconceived notions. When you do this you miss the opportunity to allow these catalytic events to begin to move you from orientation to disorientation and begin to expand your image of God.

> " What comes into our minds when we think about God is the most important thing about us. "
>
> –A. W. Tozer[1]

As we seek to cultivate and nourish Christian discernment as a way of life, it becomes critically important to have a robust image of God. If we have a limiting view of God, Christian discernment is downgraded to decision-making, calculating the pros and cons, and is quite simply no more than a practical atheism. So a healthy, expansive view of God is extremely important! But obtaining one is easier said than done.

There is a level of comfort in being able to define God, of believing you know what God will and will not do. In Exodus 3, Moses asked God for God's name. The use of a name in the Old Testament told something of the person, which is why God sometimes changed people's names. Moses was seeking to get a handle on who this God who was speaking to him was. Of course, God's response was, "I will be who I will be" (my take on I Am who I Am), and that was God's invitation to Moses to enter into a relationship, to follow God, learning through living life together. Jesus did the same in his invitation to the disciples: "follow me" (Mt. 4:19).

Exercise:

What is your current image of God? Use your journal to write or create something that captures your image of God. What words, phrases, or colors express who God is to you? Take the time to capture your image of God before moving on.

I teach a one-day class every year for a local seminary regarding the Image of God. I begin the class by passing out little wooden boxes shaped like chests, along with various colored markers, and ask the students to decorate their boxes using words and colors that convey something of their images of God. They spend about 20 minutes doing this, and many of the creations are amazing. They then share their boxes in a small group, and when they're finished, I expound about the wonder and mystery of God. I share how God is the knowable, unknowable one and that we are finite and thus incapable of fully grasping who God is. Furthermore, once we can clearly and succinctly articulate who God is, it is in that moment we have affirmed who God is not. Next, I distribute hammers and safety goggles and invite the students to SMASH their boxes as a declaration of their desire to let God be God, to fight the tendency to limit God, control God, reduce God to anything other than God, no mater how beautiful or profound. By the end of the day, most—but not all—will have broken their boxes. I understand why some do not—it's nice to have a God you know, a cozy-fire God from whom you receive comfort and support, rather than a consuming-fire God, wild and untamed. As you continue reading, I hope you will make the time and effort to explore and expand your WHO of God, as that image will free you or limit you in your desire to embody the will of God.

Exercise:

Returning to the picture of God you created in the exercise above, how might your current image limit your ability to fully and freely follow God, no matter what? How does your description of God confine God in a God-box of your own making? Are you willing to let God be God, to discover more about who God is and is not in your life journey? You might want to tear up what you wrote earlier and pray, "God I desire to know you in ever-deepening ways. Free me from my constructs that limit you, from my desire for comfort and control that keep you from being fully God."

You probably have more than one image of God: a head knowledge or theological understanding based on what you have read and been taught, but also an operational or heart image of God that shapes how you actually live. This operational image of God is formed through experiences, interactions with significant others, and life circumstances. As you continue reading, ask God to help you realize the difference between your head or theological idea of God and your operational image. Tozer writes, "Our real idea of God may be buried beneath our conventional prayers, conventional worship and conventional doctrines. To dig down to these real notions and to replace them with correct ones will require an intelligent and vigorous search and perhaps painful self-examination."[2] And I would add it is not something you do solely by your own effort but you partner with God on this journey and, if possible, have another person in your life—like a spiritual director or spiritual friend—who has navigated from orientation through disorientation and on to reorientation at least once. Yes, this is an ongoing pattern when it comes to our relationship with God—God is an ever-expanding horizon, the ever-changing unchangeable one and our life now and to come will always involve a greater and greater knowing and experiencing of the infinite, triune God.

This pursuit of a greater freedom to let God be God will entail:

- A choice—let God be God. You must be willing to hold in open hands your current image and knowing of God, not viewing them as erroneous but as incomplete (as they will always will be)—willing to experience discomfort in your relationship with God as you move from orientation to disorientation. You do not make this happen but enter into the process.

- Being aware and reflecting on what is happening in and around you and how it is impacting you—spiritually, emotionally, psychologically and processing this with God.

- Honestly interacting with God in prayer. God meets you where you are, so it is important to be honest, to express your heart, your struggles, your questions. In the book of Job, this honest type of dialogue is played out and while God never directly answers Job's questions and concerns, Job's view of God is enlarged. Job states, "Therefore I have uttered what I did not understand, things too wonderful for me, which I did not know…I had heard of you by the hearing of the ear, but now my eye sees you" (Job 42:3b, 5). Through honest and unedited dialogue, Job discovers that God is more than he had ever imagined God to be. In Job, we see this movement from orientation to disorientation, and then the arrival at reorientation.

- Paying *attention to those areas of resistance* to God, the message, words, and teachings of others, the circumstances of your life. Embrace this internal discomfort, let the questions arise, ask yourself what is no longer ringing true, what no longer seems as certain, as black and white, as it previously did. Invite God into this, and also invite a spiritual mentor or spiritual director who has traveled down this road before.

If you are open to letting God be God and willing to let go of the comfort and security that is a hallmark of being in a place of orientation, then you will begin to become aware of the opportunities to have your image of God deepened and expanded. This can be a painful and often lonely journey, as it will appear to others that you are losing your faith; your searching, honesty and questions will scare many. That is why I strongly urge you to not go down this path alone BUT do go down this path, for what you will discover about

God will change your life and help you as you seek to live Jesus and embody God's will.

GOD LOVES YOU

Earlier in the chapter, I challenged you to allow your image of God to expand and develop and to avoid relegating God to a theological box, even a beautifully adorned box. God is always more than you can think, articulate, or even imagine. But now I want to focus on one aspect of who God is: God is love. You will be invited to rest in and consider God's love for you, to move from abstract knowledge about the love of God toward personal internalization of your very own identity as one who is deeply and unconditionally loved by God. (We will explore that critical component of identity more fully in the next chapter.)

Discernment is grounded in the relational truths that God is with (within) you, knows you, cares about you, and individually loves you. These truths go beyond the "God so loved the world" mindset into claiming a personal, I-know-the-number-of-the-hairs-your-head love. The desire to include God in the comings and goings of daily life, to pay attention to and act on what the Spirit is communicating, flows from a deep and abiding sense that God stands with us and is committed to our welfare. The truth is that God loves YOU with an unconditional-nothing-can-separate-you-from-it love that is beyond your ability to fully comprehend, yet you

> " May God's love wrap and enfold you, embrace you, guide you, surround you, and bring you comfort. "
>
> –Julian of Norwich[3]

can still know it and experience it in ways that free and transform you to live Jesus, grow in Christian discernment, and desire God's will above all things.

EMBRACING GOD'S LOVE

Gordon T. Smith states, "Nothing is so fundamental to the Christian journey as knowing and feeling that we are loved (by God). Nothing...Our greatest need is to know this truth and to anchor our lives to it, living in a profound inner confidence of God's love."[4]

As you read this, you may be tempted to skip ahead, thinking you've heard it before, that the one thing you do know about God is that God loves you. If that's true, congratulations! That knowledge will serve you well moving forward, but please don't skip what follows. Paul's great desire for individuals at the church at Ephesus was that they would know the height, depth, width, and breadth of the love of Christ, a knowing that exceeded their ability to understand (Eph. 3:17–20). The subjective knowing of God's love is critical when it comes to living Jesus, embodying God's will, and embracing Christian discernment as a way of life. Many Christians may know that God loves them in their head, and believe in their heart that God loves others, but when it comes to owning and embracing God's personal love for them without reservation, they struggle.

I believe we, the Church, are to blame. We start out by declaring the amazing love of God demonstrated in and through Jesus, but as soon as one becomes a follower of Jesus, receiving forgiveness and adopted into the family, we pull the classic bait-and-switch ploy. Instead of providing the time and space to soak in God's love, to let it seep deep within the new believer's heart—embracing them in their brokenness, being a salve to their wounds, a healing balm to their shame—we immediately move on to the two great commandments of loving God and loving others, forgetting in the process that we can only love because God first loved us with a nothing-can-separate-you-from-it love. God's love is unlike any we have ever experienced, a love that needs to be internalized before moving forward. It is this amazing love that frees us from the felt need to earn it, to prove one's worth, or to seek it through the praise, admiration, and encouragement of others. It is only an experiential knowledge of God's unconditional love that frees us to engage with God in the living of life.

To further explore God's love, we turn to scripture, 1 John 4:16 (NIV), which reads, "And so we *know* and *rely* on the love God has for us. God is love. Whoever *lives* in love lives in God, and God in him (emphasis mine)."

To *know* God's love, we must differentiate between *experiencing* it and knowing *about* it. Subjective knowledge is critical, and yet it's somehow difficult for many to apply to themselves. Such knowledge begins by opening ourselves to the possibility of it. We can begin by reflecting at the end of our day, "How did I experience God's love today?" and remembering that every good gift is from heaven above. Our tendency is to look for big things, but ask God to reveal to you how God's love was demonstrated even in small ways. Maybe it was in a chance encounter with a friend, a beautiful sunset, an internal sense of wellbeing. If you make this reflection a regular practice, you will discover personal signs of God's love. When I find pennies, I am reminded of God's love and provision for me. Each time I've found a coin in the last twenty years, I've declared, "*Jehovah Jireh*, the Lord provides." Every penny I find reminds me of God's love for me.

Once you know God's love experientially, you can begin to rely on it—trusting that like gravity, God's love is always exerting its power on you, shaping and forming you from the inside out. This reliance naturally flows into living in love—partnering with God's love as the force that guides, empowers, and emboldens you to love and serve both God and others. Living in God's love fosters a shared life with God, a heart more open to God, a sensitivity to God's invitations, and a willingness to follow. Knowing, relying, and living in God's love is critical to Christian discernment, to the ability to embody and follow God's will from your heart.

STRUGGLING WITH GOD'S LOVE

Many find it extremely difficult to embrace God's love, often as a result of their own stories. As mentioned earlier, our image of God is shaped to a large degree by the interactions we've had with significant people in our lives. If you were abused, left unprotected, loved conditionally, loved imperfectly, abandoned, ignored, made to feel unlovable, unknown, and/or if love was something that was a reward for good behavior, performing at a certain level…your scars may be too deep. Your journey toward experiential knowledge of God's love will be difficult, but not impossible, and may need the help of a therapist, spiritual director, or spiritual mentor. The struggle to internalize God's love is a huge barrier to growing in one's ability to hear from God and follow God's leading. As you continue, know that God does love you and NOTHING can change that—not your sins (past and present), nothing you have done or anything that has been done to you, not your feelings, or even your unbelief. As you continue to ponder and soak in God's love, celebrate your baby steps toward believing. God loves YOU—"I believe, help me in my unbelief."

Read the poem to the right. Which words seem to speak most deeply to you? Which words do you feel resistance around? What is the invitation of this poem for you? What would keep you from owning it and living your life as one loved by God, as the beloved of God? Share your answers with God.

be loved

be

as

one

who

is

loved—

deeply,

perfectly,

tenderly,

uniquely,

powerfully,

simply,

profoundly.

GOD'S EXTRAORDINARY LOVE

You are loved by God! Can you receive those words? This love of God is not a love from afar but is a costly love that knows no bounds. Jesus embodied this love as he became sin (2 Cor. 5:21), the vilest person who ever lived, that you would be able to become the righteousness of God. And this all took place while you were sinful and an enemy of God, not when you had your act together. God's love is a transforming love that has been poured within us and over us, changing our status forever from sinner to child of God.

The truth is that God loves you with a nothing-can-separate-you-from-it-head-over-heels kind of love, an extravagant, excessive, involved love that must be expressed. One look at you and God's heart beats faster. One glance of your eyes in God's direction takes God's breath away. It is this type of love that you can never be separated from.

Reflect on the statements below. Which two are easiest for you to believe and which two are the most difficult for you to believe? What makes it challenging for you to believe?

1. God loves you. _____

2. God likes you. _____

3. God enjoys you. _____

4. You are incapable of defeating God's love for you. _____

5. God loves loving you. _____

God knows you and loves you. Let that love seep deep within you, touching those places you do not let others see, bringing the possibility of healing to the shame buried deep within, to the wounds that are toxic to you and to others. God's love is a non-discriminatory love that keeps loving you no matter what and embraces all that you are (Romans 8:1; 31–32; 38–39).

RELYING ON, LIVING IN GOD'S LOVE

As I have come to know, rely, and live my life in the light of God's love, it has fostered within me the desire to intentionally invite God into my daily life, asking God for wisdom, seeking to open my heart to the various ways God communicates to me. I've also found myself stopping to ask if I did in fact believe in that love for me, and if so, what would I do? This question often brings great clarity, freeing me from the confines of what others think, the limits of common sense, the constraints of my own insecurities and desire to please others. I have found that relying on God's love, living in light of God's love, provides the internal space to hear God, sense the prompting of the Spirit more clearly, and have the ability to choose. I can choose to embody God's will rather than automatically following others' expectations or demands. Now, I don't always choose to say yes to the invitations and challenges of God in the moment, but at least I can choose.

Also, knowing that there is no condemnation in Christ and that nothing can separate me from God, I am able to process the encounter later and reflect on what made it difficult for me to say yes to God in that particular circumstance, thus helping me to maybe say yes in the future.

As you are able to internalize God's love even a little more, you will be increasingly able to combat those internal voices and feelings that seek to condemn, that try to convince you that you are less-than. As you rely on and live in God's love, your relationship with God will deepen and flourish.

Because Christian discernment is relational at its core, it is of paramount importance that you have experiential knowing of the indescribable love God has for you, that you see God as a God who is for you, actively loving you into this moment and the next and the next, and that you know nothing will ever separate you from that love. Take time to soak in the truth of God's love for you—open up all that you are to God. Only in this experiential knowing can you even begin to trust God enough to enter into a shared life and to begin to learn and heed the ways God communicates.

EXERCISES:

1. Endeavor to bring a new level of honesty and openness as you communicate with God. Share your anger, frustration, questions, anxiety...knowing God hears you, loves you, delights in you, even likes you and that nothing you say can change that. Dare to be like Job.

2. Explore your life in terms of orientation, disorientation, and re-orientation. Where do you currently see yourself—if in orientation, enjoy the comfort and security, but be open to God moving you into a time of disorientation. If you are in disorientation, then seek to be patient with yourself, endeavoring to trust God and the process, resisting the temptation to try to get back to orientation. I would also encourage you to find another to journey with you—one who gives you freedom to be open and honest, and who does not need to rescue you or to defend God. If you are in reorientation, then enjoy this respite, embrace, and live into and out of your new learnings and discoveries about the person of God and the Christian life.

DAILY PRACTICE:

This week, practice gratitude in the morning and evening, thanking God for five to seven things each day. In the morning, answer the question "what are you grateful for as you begin this new day?" and then in the evening, "what gifts from God are you aware of as you look back over your day?"

WHO ARE YOU?

We now shift our focus from our image of God and God's love for us to exploring who we are—our identity in Christ. You may be thinking, *What does who I am in Christ have to do with discernment?* Well, just as your knowledge of God transforms the contours of your heart, helping you trust God and follow as you discern God's leading, knowing who *you* are forms and shapes what you value and how you spend your time and resources, and thus determines the decisions that you make.

At one point in my life I fancied myself a bicyclist, so I spent much time, energy, and money on my beautiful red racing bicycle—riding it, reading about riding it, and working on it. All the time and resources seemed well-spent because *I was a bicyclist*. My identity gave shape to how I lived my life. Your answer to the question, "Who are you?" is an important one, and when the answer is based on your identity in Christ, that changes everything.

When we speak of a new identity in Christ, we are not talking about a spiritual makeover, or a perfunctory pronouncement that you are merely forgiven or "not guilty." No, something profound HAS taken place within you, changing you so radically that you can rightly be called a new creation—

God's masterpiece created in Christ Jesus.

It is important to note that we are not *creating an identity,* but *discovering and owning the identity that God has already given us.* This identity is grounded in what God has done in us, from creating us in God's own image and then continuing the work of transforming us into Christlikeness that began at the point of our salvation.

> "Define yourself radically as one beloved by God. This is the true self. Every other identity is illusion."
>
> —Brennan Manning[1]

The truth of your identity is built upon the foundation of God's love. To the degree that your security and significance are grounded in the truth that you are deeply loved by God, you will be free to embrace the depth and magnitude of who you are in Christ.

Who you are in Christ recognizes the importance of Jesus' transformative acceptance of you. If you emphasize your acceptance of Jesus without acknowledging his radical acceptance of you through justification, reconciliation, and the indwelling of the Spirit, you are in danger of taking responsibility for your relationship with God, of assuming it is contingent on your actions and works. As you explore your identity, it's important to remember its foundation is in God, that it is a direct result of Jesus' life, death, and resurrection. Your identity is a declaration of God's "for-us-ness" and of Jesus' transforming acceptance of you.

Before beginning to explore who you are in Christ, I want us to look at identity as it played out in Jesus' own life. Jesus, at age 30, went to John the Baptist to be baptized. As Jesus came out of the water, he heard these words from God, "This is my beloved Son, with whom I am well pleased" (Matt. 3:17). It's easy, when looking at this story, to minimize the importance of God's affirmation of Jesus, but that affirmation really couldn't have been more timely. Jesus was rumored to be a child born out of wedlock; he grew up with whispers and finger pointing. But now, as Jesus was about to begin his ministry, God, His Father, reminded Him of his holy kinship, speaking words of love into the heart of Jesus. At this point Jesus had done no miracles, preached no sermons, had no part in ministry, and yet God affirmed his identity as Beloved Son. Jesus also heard these same powerful words on the Mount of Transfiguration. As Jesus was preparing for his journey to the cross, God once again reminded him, "This is my beloved Son,-with whom I am well pleased; listen to him" (Matthew 17:5). I believe this also happened often when Jesus would slip away to pray.

Jesus' owning of his identity was important, as it formed his character and shaped his life. His awareness of his sonship determined his yes's and no's, created a dependence on God, fostering a desire to do the will of the Father no matter what. In chapter 13 of his gospel, John states, "Jesus, knowing that the Father had given all things into his hands, and

Apart from a deep and abiding relationship with God, you have no real identity.

that he had come from God and was going back to God, rose from supper. He laid aside his outer garments, and taking a towel, tied it around his waist." Jesus' knowledge of who he was and what his life was about prompted him to specific actions. This passage confirms the role our identity can play in the Christian discernment process. As we own our identity, it helps us to live life in harmony with who God has created us to be and, like it did in Jesus, fosters in us the desire to embody God's will.

Given the importance of our identity, it's not surprising that it comes under attack from Satan, as he seeks to create questions and doubts. We see this in the life of Jesus. Immediately after his baptism, the Spirit (more about the critical role of the Spirit in Chapter 8) led Jesus into the wilderness for a forty-day fast, during which Satan appeared to tempt him. In the first two temptations, Satan said to Jesus, "If you are the son of God..." (Matthew 4:3, 4:6). In essence, Satan was questioning Jesus' identity as the beloved of God and asking him to prove it. We, like Jesus, can be tempted in regards to our identity, tempted to forget or lose sight of who we are, to take on an external identity that is not who we were created to be, but which can nonetheless form and shape us. It is too easy to let our roles—mom, father, teacher, police officer, pastor—morph into identities that begin to shape us, rather than claiming and nurturing our deeper, unchangeable identity in Christ. As we own the identity that is already ours in Christ, we can begin to shed the roles and expectations of the world and our own making.

Below you are invited to prayerfully consider the unchangeable components of your identity in Christ, the characteristics that are yours as a result of the life, death and resurrection of Jesus. These truths belong to you and cannot be taken away.

1. one who is forgiven by God

2. one who is justified

3. one who is sanctified

4. one who is adopted by God

5. one who belongs to God

6. one who contains God

7. one who is the beloved of God

Pause a moment and think about what each of the above statements communicates regarding your God-given identity. Write a couple of words or sentences that express what each means to you. Which of these characteristics are you most drawn to/most resistant to? Why? Is this an identity that is currently forming and shaping your life?

WHO ARE YOU?

One who is FORGIVEN by God: Forgiveness frees you from being defined by your past, but it is not enough to know you are forgiven. *Accepting* your forgiveness in Christ is an important step in freeing you to be who God has created you to be.

I have come to picture the word forgiveness as a gift basket containing the goodies of God's grace. But before looking at the goodies of God's grace, everything else on the list above that comprise our unchangeable identity, please take time to consider the following verses on forgiveness, paying attention to the thoughts and feelings that surface:

> *"For as high as the heavens are above the earth, so great is his steadfast love toward those who fear him; as far as the east is from the west, so far does he remove our transgressions from us." –Psalm 103:11-12*

> *"I will remember their sins and their lawless deeds no more." –Hebrews 10:17b*

> *"I, I am he who blots out your transgressions for my own sake, and I will not remember your sins" –Isaiah 43:25*

These three verses speak of the extraordinary nature of God's forgiveness. Your sins are not covered up but removed, blotted out, and remembered no more. If God has done this for you, you can no longer hold your sins against yourself. They no longer matter. You have been radically changed. You are forgiven!

One who is JUSTIFIED by God: The words justified/justification can be a tad intimidating, but they speak to a theological concept that is important to understand. Justification communicates what God has declared to be true about you—You are righteous and holy, which is not surprising since forgiveness implies God forgetting ALL of your sins.

Some like to hold on to their past identity as a sinner as a badge of humility, or out of fear they will become prideful, but God must certainly be perplexed by this. God declares that in Christ we are forgiven and justified, standing before God unashamed. We can open the door to God's presence and climb into God's lap, knowing we are accepted, loved and delighted in. It can be no other way! God no longer sees us as sinners, but justified through union with Jesus, righteous and holy. Seeking to make yourself worthy is an affront to God's free and gracious gift of justification.

Personally I have been a bit confused by the idea of justification in the past. It seemed like I was being let off on a technicality. Although really guilty, as a result of some clerical error or procedural loophole, I was let go. God was okay with it, but everyone else still saw me as guilty. It turns out that I was confused because I was totally wrong. The truth is that because of the death and resurrection of Jesus, the righteousness of Jesus has been given to us, resulting in us being fully accepted—we are no longer sinners, but holy ones, saints, and children of God. *"For our sake he made him to be sin who knew no sin, so that in him we might become the righteousness of God."* (2 Cor. 5:21)

You, now and forever, stand before God (not cowering behind Jesus, but standing upright before God) without blemish. Accept it! Celebrate! When the truth of your justification is embraced, it releases you from the need or inclination to try to earn something from God.

One who is SANCTIFIED (and being sanctified) by God: Another intimidating theological term, but I promise this is the last one. Justification and sanctification can never be separated, because God who justifies also sanctifies; they are two sides of the same coin. Both are essential elements of salvation resulting from the death and resurrection of Jesus. Justification changes your standing by saying you are righteous and accepted by God (Romans 5); sanctification changes and is changing you—it is an ongoing process. Sin is no longer your master! You have a new God-given capacity to experience God relationally: to follow God, honor God, hear God, love God, and say yes to God.

As I reflect on this new capacity, I am reminded of Spiderman, the comic-book hero. Spiderman's abilities are a result of something that happened to him: being bitten by a radioactive spider. This occurrence caused his transformation, and he was radically changed. The challenge for him was how to make use of his new capabilities and then decide how to employ them—for good or for evil. Similarly, as Christians, we have a new capacity, a radically changed capacity—a capacity unavailable outside of unity in Christ. This new capacity allows us to choose to not let sin reign in us, not obey its lusts, but to walk in newness of life and live Jesus. No longer slaves to sin, we are now free to choose life and able to embody God's will, to live God's will from our hearts.

One who is ADOPTED by God: You were once outside the family of God, but now you are a child of God, joint heir with Christ. You are God's precious child, uniquely loved, valued, and cherished. This kinship is a precious piece of our identity, at least it is for me. Adopted at birth, I never really felt as if my family got me, never felt fully one with my adopted sister or my parents. There was always something missing, something not clicking. When I became a Christian at age seventeen and then discovered this imagery of adoption in the context of God, it spoke deeply to my heart. I realized that in the family of God I was being adopted by my true Father, the one who gave me life, the one who knows me better than I know myself.

Your adoption by God is a homecoming. God your creator is, has been, and always will be your Abba, your Father, your daddy who knows you intimately and profoundly understands and appreciates you. You can cry out, "ABBA, FATHER" without hesitation or second-guessing. You are God's beloved child and God is your loving daddy.

Paul expresses this in Romans 8:15–17: "For you did not receive the spirit of slavery to fall back into fear, but you have received the Spirit of adoption as sons, by whom we cry, 'Abba! Father!' The Spirit himself bears witness with our spirit that we are children of God, and if children, then heirs—heirs of God and fellow heirs with Christ…" What a wonderful reminder of the truth of our adoption by God! We are no longer slaves to fear, but children of God, heirs of God and co-heirs with Christ.

I love what Eugene Petersen does with this passage in *The Message*, "This resurrection life you received from God is not a timid, grave-tending life. It's adventurously expectant, greeting God with a childlike 'What's next, Papa?' God's Spirit touches our spirits and confirms who we really are. We know who he is, and we know who we are: Father and children." As we own our identity as children of God, it births a risk-taking, adventurous spirit along with a confident expectation that our Father is for us, and there is nothing to worry about. It is this confident relational connection with God that stimulates an excited yearning to discern and follow God.

One who BELONGS to God: As a Christian you are not your own; you are God's very possession, one of God's people, formed by God for God's own self. Bound up in your belonging to God and living for God is your need to be yielded to God, dependent on God, seeking to live as Jesus lived and wanting God's will over your own. As you read these sentences and the following verses, what feelings/thoughts arise within you? Are you resistant to these truths, drawn to them, challenged by them? Why? Express your thoughts and feelings to God.

> *"For none of us lives to himself, and none of us dies to himself. For if we live, we live to the Lord, and if we die, we die to the Lord. So then, whether we live or whether we die, we are the Lord's." –Romans 14:7–8*

> *"In him you also, when you heard the word of truth, the gospel of your salvation, and believed in him, were sealed with the promised Holy Spirit, who is the guarantee of our inheritance until we acquire possession of it, to the praise of his glory." –Ephesians 1:13–14*

One who CONTAINS God: This is a mystery that takes time to get one's heart and head around: God lives in you, you are a container of God, a home for God. This is every bit as mind boggling as Mary carrying Jesus, the creator of all that is seen and unseen, within her womb. Reflect on the reality of God living in you—that even as you live, move and have your being in God, God lives moves and has God's being in you, in me—WOW! If you truly believed that God has taken up residence in you, how would that change how you lived life?

Read the verses below, paying attention to what thoughts and feelings surface within you as you sit with and ponder the astonishing mystery of God taking up residence within you.

Chapter Four: Who Are You?

"Do you not know that you are God's temple and that God's Spirit dwells in you?" –1 Corinthians 3:16

"If the Spirit of him who raised Jesus from the dead dwells in you, he who raised Christ Jesus from the dead will also give life to your mortal bodies through his Spirit who dwells in you." –Romans 8:11

"Jesus answered him, 'If anyone loves me, he will keep my word, and my Father will love him, and we will come to him and make our home with him.'" –John 14:23

"You, however, are not in the flesh but in the Spirit, if in fact the Spirit of God dwells in you. Anyone who does not have the Spirit of Christ does not belong to him." –Romans 8:9

One who is the BELOVED of God: This identity piece flows out of being one uniquely and profoundly loved by God (i.e., the focus of the previous chapter). God loves you to death and as a result you are the beloved of God. It's who you are—one distinctively loved by God—the beloved of God. This may be a particularly difficult truth for you to accept but it is important to own it. Your identity as the beloved of God is at the core of all the other components. As you accept, know, rely on, live into and out of your identity as the beloved of God, your desire to embody God's will is fueled. Your heart is prepared for a different way of life. Your identity as the beloved of God is the pinnacle of who you are in Christ—it affirms the radically transforming power of Jesus' acceptance of you. Your identity as the beloved of God is the sun of your identity galaxy, exerting power over all the other planets, keeping them in proper alignment.

"Put on then, as God's chosen ones, holy and beloved..."
–Colossians 3:12a

WHO YOU ALSO ARE—IN THE FLESH

As stated above, our core identity is who we are in Christ, end of story. This is our identity, but Paul also reminds us that we are still in a battle. Paul, reflecting on his own life, writes, "For I do not do the good I want, but the evil I do not want is what I keep on doing. Now if I do what I do not want, it is no longer I who do it, but sin that dwells within me" (Rom. 7:19–20). Also, in Galatians 5, he delineates the ongoing battle between the flesh (inner predisposition to sin, toward self-gratification) and the Spirit of God within us. As stated above, we are sanctified and we are being sanctified, but we are not yet fully the creatures we one day will be, and as a result we are in a battle. It is important to remember, as Paul points out above, that even in the midst of the battle we are still who we are in Christ—*"it is no longer I who do it"*—Paul is claiming the deepest reality of who he is in Christ. Our identity in Christ is unchangeable.

It is important to note this battle when we're talking about discernment, for we each need to acknowledge the predispositions and proclivities that can hinder us from recognizing the communications of God, the subtle promptings of the Spirit, or even the desire to follow what we come to know. These predispositions, if unknown, definitely hinder our ability to freely and fully hear from God and to follow the leading of the Spirit. However, if we know and name our "stuff," then we can be aware of the internal pulls or resistance against following God and we can factor that in as we seek to embody God's will.

A book I found personally helpful in this area is *Signature Sins*, by Michael Mangis. This book helped me to explore the seven deadly sins and then name and own the sins I tend to continually struggle with. This process has been helpful as I have sought to discern God's leading and to respond to the promptings of the Holy Spirit. For, now I know that there are certain invitations from God that I am not readily open to, and I can factor that in as I seek to honestly follow God and embrace holy indifference (see Chapter 5).

This awareness of our brokenness is not about condemnation, but about helping ourselves not be subconsciously enslaved to these tendencies. Instead, we want to be aware of their power and influence so that we can more readily be free to say yes to God and live into and out of who God has created, called, and declared us to be.

As we own God's love for us and embrace our unchangeable identity in Christ, we become free to look at and name those things within ourselves with which we continue to struggle, that sometimes still shape our values and our worldview, and that can make it difficult to fully follow as God leads us. We are free to pray the prayer of David, found in Psalm 139:23–24, "Search me, O God, and know my heart! Try me and know my thoughts! And see if there be any grievous way in me, and lead me in the way everlasting!"

FINAL THOUGHTS

The embracing of your identity in Christ is critically important when it comes to your ability to discern and then to follow as God leads. As stated earlier, your identity is discovered by you, not created by you. All the characteristics we discussed above are true of who you are, but the challenge is to order your life in light of these truths. Just as Jesus battled to hold onto his identity, so will you. The world, the evil one, and other people will seek to convince you that these identity pieces aren't true, don't matter, or can be replaced by a myriad of worldly roles. Your true identity and measure of worth can only be found in God and in who you are as God's new creation, God's masterpiece: forgiven, justified, sanctified (and being sanctified), adopted by God, belonging to God, containing God, the beloved of God.

As you embrace whose you are, and who you are, it begins to shape the contours of your heart in ways that enlarge a desire for God—the things and ways of God. It propels you to live Jesus and positions you to begin to distinguish good from evil, perceive the best from the good, recognize the communications of God, and embody God's will. This naturally flows from a life soaking in God's love.

EXERCISES:

1. Which one of the truths of who you are—forgiven, justified, sanctified, adopted, belonging, containing, beloved—are you most drawn to?

2. Which one the seven identity truths listed above are most difficult to get your heart and head around?

3. Which one the seven identity truths listed above do you sense God inviting you to more fully embrace? Why might this be?

DAILY PRACTICE:

This week begin to pray the Prayer of Recollection each day. You will find this prayer in appendix. The Prayer of Recollection is designed to help you to begin to embrace and live out who you are—your unchangeable identity. The video for Chapter 4 will walk you through the steps of this prayer. Go to www.b-ing.org and click on "Christian Discernment." Please make this a part of the beginning of your day for the next several weeks.

CHAPTER FIVE

BE FREE

God loves loving you! God is loving you into this moment and the next and the next and the next. And you—you are a new creation, forgiven, adopted, chosen. These twin truths, "whose you are and who you are," form the foundation upon which the focus of this chapter is built: indifference.

The word *indifference* makes many Christians feel uneasy when it is associated with the Christian life, as it conjures up images of unconcern, disinterest, a distancing from the hurt and pain of others. This discomfort may be heightened when I tell you that indifference is a key trait in Jesus' character—a trait that enabled him to live totally dependent on and fully yielded to the will of God. Indifference, or as I will refer to it—*holy indifference*—is a critical component when it comes to our ability to discern and to make God-honoring decisions.

WHAT IS HOLY INDIFFERENCE?

Holy indifference is a means of spiritual freedom. Holy indifference is about *freedom from* and *freedom to*. It is a *freedom from* disordered attachments—those loves, needs, and desires that exert power over you, that enslave you, and it is a *freedom to* say yes to God no matter what. The reason we call these overmastering loves, needs, and desires "disordered attachments" is because they exert power over your life—a power and level of control that belongs to God alone and that can hinder you from following God. Holy indifference frees you to hear from God, to follow God, and to pursue your God given desires—those desires most true to who God has called and created you to be. While holy indifference is a synonym for freedom, disordered attachments (disordered loves), is a synonym for bondage and/or enslavement.

You may be surprised to learn there is a link between holy indifference and desire, especially passionate desire, for often when the word "indifference" is used it raises images of apathy, not caring. Holy indifference is different from common indifference. Holy indifference is about a freeing of desire, not a freedom from desire. Holy indifference has to do with a refocusing and a refining of one's desire so that a person can escape the false contests for significance, value, worth, and the cotton-candy pleasures this world offers, and embrace instead the deepest desires of one's heart: to live Jesus, to embody God's will. Through holy indifference, an individual begins to develop new eyes to see and a heart able and willing to discern the temporal from the eternal, the spiritual from the mundane, the best from the good. They discover the life-transforming truth that the finite is infinitely incapable of fulfilling our God-given core desires.

Holy indifference is an attitude that does not desire to cling to one thing over another but seeks to be open to whatever comes, discerning God's invitation/challenge/communications in each event and circumstance of life. It's about freedom to live the kind of life where you can, at any moment, say yes to God, the freedom to give something or someone up or not. What matters is the ability to respond to the promptings of God and seek to choose whatever will lead to greater honor and glory for God, to say yes to God no matter what. Holy indifference is not simply self-renunciation; it is an opting for God's will above all else.

Holy indifference is seen in the prayer Jesus taught his disciples. He began with a declaration of God as Father, implying God's love, care, power, authority, and that we are the children of God. Out of this knowing flows the desire that God's kingdom come and God's will be done in the here-and-now of our lives. The ability to have holy indifference flows out of this deep knowing of who God is and who we are, and out of a passionate desire for God's will to be done.

We see an example of holy indifference in Philippians 4:12: "I know how to be brought low, and I know how to abound. In any and every circumstance, I have learned the secret of facing plenty and hunger, abundance and need." Paul was able to be present to God regardless of his circumstances and this constant awareness led to him penning many of the letters that comprise the New Testament. Holy indifference freed him from the constraints of his circumstances, because he was not attached in a disorderly way to his need for freedom, comfort, and action; but even in prison, he was free to recognize the communications of God and to embody God's will.

WHAT DOES HOLY INDIFFERENCE LOOK LIKE?

Prime examples of holy indifference are seen in the attitudes of Jesus, Mary, and Joseph. Mary's holy indifference is humbly stated in the words, "I am the servant of the Lord; let it be to me according to your word." (Luke 1:38b). Mary did not regard her plans for marriage above God's call. She showed holy indifference to her future and thus was free to say yes to God's invitation. Joseph had his plan too. He decided to send Mary away quietly, but God communicated to him in a dream and, like Mary, Joseph let go of his plan and responded to God's leading. Jesus embodies holy indifference in the garden when he struggled with his journey to the cross. Sweating drops of blood, expressing his heart to God, he then concluded with the words, "not my will, but yours [God's], be done" (Luke 22:42b). These examples of holy indifference flow out of trust in God based on a deep knowing of the "for-us-ness" of God, a knowledge of our unchangeable identity in Christ, a valuing of God and the things of God, and a willingness to yield to God.

A more current example of holy difference is expressed in the traditional marriage vows, "...for better or worse, for richer or poorer, in sickness and in health." Here the pledge is to remain in the marriage come what may; the circumstances of life will not be the determining factor regarding faithfulness in the covenant the couple is making.

This is not to say that holy indifference precludes having or even stating a preference in our circumstances, but when push comes to shove, the desire for God's kingdom come, God's will be done, will be pivotal in the choice to be made. Even Jesus and Paul boldly stated their preferences. Jesus expressed to God his desire to not die on the cross, while Paul declared, "I am hard pressed between the two. My desire is to depart and be with Christ, for *that* is far better (emphasis mine)" (Phil. 1:23). Jesus desired to live while Paul desired to die, but each of those desires was a preference, not a demand. Each voiced a heartfelt desire that was accompanied by a holy indifference, ultimately requesting that not their wills, but God's will be done.

Holy indifference is not just acquiescing to God's will, but making a declaration of a deeper desire to embody the will of God no matter what—to live God's will from the heart. This same combination of stated preference and holy indifference is expressed by Paul in 2 Cor. 12:8–9, "Three times I pleaded with the Lord about this [Paul's thorn in the flesh], that it should leave me. But he said to me, 'My grace is sufficient for you, for my power is made perfect in weakness.' Therefore I will boast all the more gladly of my weaknesses, so that the power of Christ may rest upon me." *Holy indifference* creates a place of openness to the present reality of the moment, free of demands that accompany disordered attachments/loves/felt needs. It allows me, you, an individual, to enter each moment as an encounter with God.

What is a disordered attachment?

As stated above, a synonym for *holy indifference* is *freedom* while a synonym for *disordered attachment* would be *bondage*. Disordered attachments enslave us. The best definition I have come across for of a disordered attachment is from Anthony de Mello, "a state of clinging that comes from the false belief that something or someone is necessary for your happiness."[1]

The above definition brings to mind the storied method of trapping monkeys. The trap consists of a hollowed-out gourd with an opening just large enough for a monkey's open paw. A type of food monkeys are partial to is placed in the gourd, and a vine is attached to the gourd and to a stake firmly fixed in the ground.

The monkey smells the treat and reaches in the gourd to grasp it. However, since the opening is just large enough for the monkey's open paw, it is too small for the removal of a clenched paw. No matter how much the monkey tries to escape, it remains caught until the treat is released. Similarly, the disordered attachment keeps us prisoner as long as we tightly hold on.

A disordered attachment/love usurps the place of God in a person's life. Instead of looking to God and loving God with all one's mind, heart, and strength, we choose to run toward the felt need or desire. While a disordered attachment may not be evil in itself—in fact is often something that started off as good (relationship, children, providing for family, health, security, shelter, safety)—it becomes disordered when it takes a place of supremacy in one's life, a place that should be reserved for God alone. These disordered attachments/loves often block our ability to connect with God, creating a spiritual blindness.

One of the greatest hindrances to one's ability to discern is nicely summed up by Paul in Philippians 2:21, "For they all seek after their own interests, not those of Christ Jesus" (NASB). When our interests are elevated above the interests of Jesus or the will of God, we can know those interests are disordered attachments which will impede us from embodying God's will.

How is a disordered attachment/love formed? Author Anthony De Mello describes a three-stage process:

First comes a contact with something that gives you pleasure...Then comes the desire to hold on to it, to repeat the gratifying sensation that this thing or person caused you. Finally comes the conviction that you

will not be happy without this person or thing, you have equated the
pleasure it brings you with happiness.[2]

There is nothing wrong with finding pleasure; God has given us all things to enjoy. The problem comes when we move beyond liking or enjoying and now crave possession. It is no longer a gift to enjoy, but something that owns us. An insidious shift has taken place.

A telling sign that something has moved from preference to disordered attachment is the level of emotion that arises when we are not able to have or hold on to the person or thing that we desire. If it is a preference and we are at a place of holy indifference, it may still be difficult to let it go, as it was with Jesus in the garden when he prayed to avoid the cross. We might wish for a different outcome, but we are able to ultimately desire God's will. If we are dealing with a disordered attachment/love, we will experience intense anger, fear of loss, fear of not getting what we want, strong disappointment, and pervasive sadness. All these emotions will surface and we will not be able to let it go; the disordered desire holds on to us as much as we hold on to it.

CONCERN ABOUT OPINIONS OF OTHERS

One of the most difficult of the disordered attachments that entangles is the desire to please others, be thought highly of, liked or admired by others. Remember, preferring to be well-thought-of is not a problem in itself. The issue is when that desire becomes a controlling force. Jesus condemned the desire of the Pharisees for the approval of man in John—"they loved the glory that comes from man more than the glory that comes from God" (John 12:43)—and even attributes their unbelief to this particular disordered attachment. "How can you believe, when you receive glory from one another and do not seek the glory that comes from the only God?" (John 5:44). Commenting on his own stance regarding approval of others, Jesus states, "I do not receive glory from people" (John 5:41). Paul, echoing the words of Jesus, writes to the church at Thessalonica, "…we have been approved by God to be entrusted with the gospel, so we speak, not to please man, but to please God who tests our hearts... Nor did we seek glory from people, whether from you or from others..." (1 Thess. 2:4b, 6a). Here we see Paul owning who he is, approved by God, and the result is indifference to pleasing anyone else but God.

This holy indifference (freedom) from the power of the opinions of others and the desire to please is very difficult to escape. Once at the beginning of a weekend retreat I was leading, I noticed a man walk in and take a seat in the front row. Recognizing him, I was suddenly overcome by fear. Panic began to arise within me as I realized that I really cared about what this person would think of my message. As I internally wrestled, a breath prayer rose from the depth of my spirit and I heard myself say/breathe, "Forget Tim (not his real name); God LOVES me!" The focal point of this prayer is on the empowerment of God's love for me and my identity as the beloved of God, not the identity of the other person. This I now realize was a prayer of holy indifference, a prayer reminding me of my true identity and that God was with me and for me. It clearly does not matter what Tim or anyone else thinks of me. Through this prayer, I have found freedom to be me, to live and to share as God leads me. This is the freedom of holy indifference.

When our disordered attachment is tied to the feelings, thoughts, and words of others, it is a manifestation of our deep need to be loved, cared for, valued, and praised; and our interactions become transactions. In a real sense, we begin to approach each person or group holding out a beggar's bowl, desperately needing another to fill it with whatever makes us happy, secure, significant, loved. And if we do not receive what we're longing for, we will leave that encounter more impoverished than when we arrived. A disordered attachment hinders our ability to freely love another—to turn the other cheek, to pray for those who persecute us, to love as God loves. The unbridled desire to receive praise from others also opens us to the power of criticism. Holy indifference to both praise and criticism allows us to receive them in truth and, with God's help, to gain the insight intended.

TWO WAYS TO HANDLE DISORDERED ATTACHMENTS

1. Make it your personal mission to discover and destroy your disordered attachments. While this kind of merciless self-discovery is possible, it's also dangerous. The most predictable outcome is mere sin management, and you may end up actually harming your soul.

OR

2. Turn your eyes on the Triune God, focusing on God's love for you, presence with you, and delight in you—opening the eyes of your heart to what God reveals to be those things that keep you from being more fully the person God created you to be.

The good news is that when God shows you something that you need to work on, a particular disordered attachment, it's a cause for celebration and NOT condemnation. For when God reveals something to you, it's an invitation to greater freedom; it means you are ready to deal with this issue and it means God is committed to partnering with you in this endeavor.

CULTIVATING INDIFFERENCE

To begin, we turn our focus to God. Eugene Peterson, in *The Message*, says it well in his version of Matthew 6:33–34: "So *steep* your life in God-reality, God-initiative, God-provisions… (emphasis mine)"

I love the use of "steep" in this passage; it brings to mind brewing tea, lowering the tea ball into the water and watching the tea slowly seep out, permeating the water and releasing its fragrant aroma into the air. If you sense a longing for a greater brewing of God's love in your heart, for a freedom from disordered attachments that hamper you from living into and out of who God has created you to be, ask God's help as you reflect on God's amazing love for you.

As God leads you in the way of holy indifference, you will begin to experience the heart and mindset expressed at the end of Psalm 73: "Whom have I in heaven but you? And there is nothing on earth that I desire besides you.

My flesh and my heart may fail, but God is the strength of my heart and my portion forever...But for me it is good to be near God; I have made the Lord God my refuge, that I may tell of all your works." Nothing else matters.

Holy indifference flows from the internalized knowledge of whose you are and who you are, freeing you from disordered attachments and uncovering and fostering a deep desire for God and the embodying of God's will. That desire for God, in turn, creates the willingness to ask for God's guidance and direction and opens the way for internal awareness, which is the subject of the next chapter.

If you are holy indifferent you are free:

1. to be who God has created you to be without pretense and to invite others to do the same.

2. to love without strings attached (no beggar's bowl).

3. to be released from preoccupation with the things we can see, taste, and touch.

4. to recognize the communications of God.

5. to say yes to God—"not my will but God's will be done."

EXERCISES:

1. Below is a list of a number of areas people often need to explore in terms of disordered attachments. Slowly move over the list, asking God to reveal to you areas where you may need to apply the discipline of detachment. How do each of these become destructive desires that lead you away from God rather than to God?

- *The need to be in control*
- *The need to be right*
- *The need to be liked*
- *The need to rescue/help/serve others*
- *The need to be understood and appreciated*
- *The need to be perfect—to "do it right"*
- *The need to be comfortable*
- *The need to be healthy*
- *The need to be held in high esteem/thought well of by others*
- *The need to be happy*
- *The need to be pain-free*
- *The need for financial security*

What is the core desire (attention, affection, control, security, comfort, belonging, significance, power) you are seeking to fill with these finite resources? Ask God to help you explore God's core desires and then begin to release your core desires to God.

2. It is not what you own that you must discard, but that which owns you. Look at your life: use of time, resources, relationships, daily life, and ask yourself some hard questions:

- *What consumes my thoughts and plans?*
- *What holds my allegiance?*
- *Who or what tells me who I am?*
- *What gives me security and comfort?*
- *What makes me feel whole and complete?*
- *Who/what meets my deepest needs?*

Ask God to show you what need you're seeking to meet through each of these.

Ask God what God is asking you to do with each of these. Write down what you hear from God and then write a prayer expressing your commitment and need for God's help as you move forward into greater freedom.

3. Imagine yourself coming before Jesus as the rich young ruler (Matthew 19:16ff). After some initial interaction you say to Jesus, "What else must I do?" Jesus looks deep within your heart and says, "I want you to..." Sit before Jesus and listen for his words to you. Asked Jesus to help you discover the underlying, core desire of your disordered attachment and the help needed to escape your enslavement to it.

CHAPTER SIX

BE AWARE

The title of this chapter is "be aware" not "beware." The word *beware* indicates impending danger, whereas to *be aware* invites attentiveness to what is. The difference between these two postures of living is captured well in *The Message's* translation of Romans 8:15: "This resurrection life you have received from God is not a timid, grave-tending life [a beware life]. It's adventurously expectant [a be-aware life], greeting God with a childlike 'What's next, Papa?'" This "be aware" life is characterized by a belief that God is up to something and by a corresponding desire to join in. This "be aware" life, like the ability to be indifferent, is grounded in the knowledge of whose we are and who we are.

The importance of being aware cannot be stressed enough. As you develop the ability to be aware, to be present, to experience God in the here and now of life, you will grow in your ability to recognize the communications of God, whatever form they may take. Being aware plants you in the present moment—the only place one can experience God. While we can see God's hand in the past and pray for spiritual intervention in the future, we can only actually *be* in the present. To live in the present moment takes awareness, the ability to be present to the Presence that surrounds you (in God we live, move, and have our being), indwells you, and opens you up to God's leading and the Spirit's prompting.

Spiritual awareness is not relegated to your external world, but also involves your internal self, the stirrings of your heart. It is this internal awareness that helps us be present to the Presence that is always present to us. By integrating practices that help us pay attention to the internal promptings of the Spirit, we begin to recognize the communications of God and can then choose to live life embodying God's will.

Scripture gives us many examples of people being led by God, not while wrestling with decisions, but simply while going about their daily lives. Noah was not praying about the possibility of building an ark; Abraham was not contemplating a move to the suburbs; David not discerning if he should be king; Gideon not dreaming of becoming a judge; Mary not considering pregnancy; Paul not wrestling with his faith. In each of these cases, God's life-changing message came in the midst of daily life, changing not only the individual but all of history.

How aware are you as you journey through a day? How many times do you see without really seeing, hear without listening, travel through life on auto-pilot? Generally we are everywhere but where we are—on our way to the next appointment or event, on a journey that never ends. Our phones, schedules, and pace all conspire to keep us unaware. Even when something momentarily awakens our awareness, we often choose to capture the scene by clicking a picture with our ubiquitous cameras, rather than opening to the moment—opening to God in the moment. I do not think it a coincidence that Jesus' desire was for his followers to have eyes to see and ears to hear. It is noteworthy that Jesus also closes each of his messages to the seven churches of Revelation with the words, "He who has an ear, let him hear what the Spirit says to the churches" (Rev. 2:7a).

An excellent illustration of the nuances of awareness is found in Exodus 3, when Moses notices a burning bush. This life-altering moment took place not as Moses was praying or wrestling with a decision, but while he was tending sheep, something he had been doing for about 40 years. But this day something new caught his attention. The passage reads, "And the angel of the Lord appeared to him in a flame of fire out of the midst of a bush. He looked, and behold, the bush was burning, yet it was not consumed" (3:2). Moses noticed something, but this first level of awareness was not the crucial act. The next verse contains the necessary additional step of awareness: "And Moses said, 'I will turn aside to see this great sight, why the bush is not burned.'" Moses' awareness moved him beyond noticing and into an action. He turned aside from his duties to see what was happening. And then we read, "When the Lord saw that he turned aside to see, God called to him out of the bush…" (3:4a). It was not merely passing curiosity about the bush that mattered to God, but that Moses turned aside, choosing to be present in the moment. That is when God spoke to Moses, not before. True awareness moves beyond simply noticing and turns you aside to enter into and to be fully aware of that which initially caught your attention—a sunset, a song, a passage of scripture, poetry, a word spoken by another, an inner prompting…

God surrounds us, indwells us, and we are invited to be constantly and consciously aware in order to embody God's will, to be open to encountering the living God in whom we live, move, and have our being. But we often settle for the routine, the expected, the banal. What if we began to think of our world, our everyday circumstances, as a possible opportunity for an encounter with God? In the words of Elizabeth Browning, "Earth's crammed with heaven, / And every common bush afire with God, / But only he who sees takes off his shoes; / The rest sit round and pluck blackberries."[1]

THE PRESENT MOMENT: FROM NOWHERE TO *NOW HERE*

As stated above, the only place and time we can encounter or experience God is in the present moment. As creatures of time, unable to travel to the past or the future, it is in the "now here" of this moment that we live. It is only in the now here that we are able to know, experience, and walk with Jesus. Thus, it behooves us to be aware of what is happening around us and within us in this moment. The question in each moment is always the same, "Will I be open to God and self, seeking to be aware, knowing this is a time and place to encounter God? Or will I maintain my self-determined course with its responsibilities, demands, and fleeting promises of worth, significance, and security?"

Jean-Pierre de Caussade wrote a book dealing with this important perspective entitled, *Abandonment to Divine Providence*. His premise is that God's will for us is discovered and lived into in the moment that we find ourselves—the present moment, the now here of our lives.[2]

With a willing heart and attentiveness to the now here, we can learn to recognize God's communications and the Spirit's lead. When we are preoccupied or otherwise unable to be aware of the present, it can feel like we are nowhere, that the moment is a meaningless waste of time. An assortment of emotions intensify with each failed attempt to escape perceived purposelessness, wasted effort, even hopelessness. But when we choose to embrace the *present moment,* to be open to and aware of it as it is, we are more likely to hear from God, see God, and be touched by God. The now here is the place of encounter.

I can't count the conversations I have had, the times I have prayed with people, the rest and refreshment I have experienced when I was *able to see a disruption to my plans as a gift/opportunity to experience God, myself, and others.* As we are able to embrace the moment rather than deny it, control it, or bemoan it, we can challenge the feelings of meaninglessness, frustration and impatience that may arise. We are *able to walk through the now here with God, even though it may be dark and foreboding.* God is with us and within us, loving us into each moment full of power, wisdom, and grace; God is for us in ways that we cannot begin to fathom. This knowledge, when combined with the deep knowing that we are the beloved of God, frees us to hear from God and walk with God, embracing the unforced rhythms of God's grace (Matt. 11, *The Message*) come what may.

The willingness to live with a growing awareness of the present moment is founded on the twin truths about who God is and who you are as the be-loved of God. This internalized awareness of the power, love, grace, faithful-ness of God, and God's personal involvement in your life, combined with a foundational identity as the beloved of God, creates an expectant awareness in the present moment, the now here of life. It is upon this foundation that we can build the practices critical to creating the internal space in our heart that fosters the ability to be aware in the moment—to transform the feelings of nowhere that are often associated with the present. Just as the difference between nowhere and now here is just a little space between the *w* and the *h*, so it is in our lives; the creation of a little internal space makes all the differ-ence when it comes to living Jesus—embodying God's will from our heart.

THE THREE S'S OF AWARENESS: SLOWING, SOLITUDE, SILENCE

It is the three S's of awareness that cultivate the internal space necessary to embrace the now here of life, the present moment. These three practices help you listen and behold, externally and internally, with new ears and new eyes—ears able to recognize the communications of God and eyes that see beyond the temporal to the eternal (2 Cor. 4:18) and respond accordingly.

The first S of awareness is *slowing down*, which is contrary to how we tend to live. Our lives move at a frenetic pace—a blur of driven-ness and relentless activity. We wear busyness as a badge, boasting of our importance, worthiness, and productivity. It is not surprising that daydreaming and idle-ness are viewed negatively. No one has ever lost a job because they have worked too long or too hard. The tireless workers who go above and beyond are the ones who get awards and promotions. Slowing down isn't easy, but it is critical when it comes to cultivating awareness and learning to hear and recognize the communications of God.

In Psalm 46:10 the psalmist addresses this need to slow down and con-nects it to knowing and experiencing God. The Psalmist writes: "Be still, and know that I am God" (NIV); "Cease striving and know that I am God" (NASB); "Step out of the traffic!" (*The Message*). Each of these translations speaks to the importance of slowing down and two of them emphasize the need to extricate oneself from the busyness of life in order to experience God. Anyone who chooses to follow Jesus and seriously desires to embody God's will must first slow down. Slowing is part of the rhythm of creation, as seen in the division of a day into day and night, the giving of the Sabbath, and the seasons of a year—fall and winter being times of rest in nature. Yet we humans have gone out of our way to create activities that keep us going no matter what. All our labor-saving devices have not provided us times for rest, but for more productivity; vacations and weekends are not used as times to rest, but are filled with endless activity. Jokingly, people talk about needing to go back to work to rest up from their weekend, or needing a vacation from their vacation. All this activity robs us of the ability to be aware, to notice, to turn aside.

Becoming aware involves slowing down, even though it may feel all wrong. Consider the difference between driving and walking through your neighborhood. As you walk, you see things and have the opportunity for conversations or observations you could never experience from your speeding car. As you slow your pace of life, you are able to notice, to encounter, to be aware in ways not formerly possible. One of my favorite places in the United States is the magnificent Grand Tetons. I think one of the reasons I am so taken with them is that I first experienced their beauty while slowly riding my bicycle across the United States. Each day I rode next to those incredible mountains, watching them change with the movements of the sun and clouds. I was awestruck—at times it seemed like I wasn't even moving. The unhurried pace allowed the experience to settle deep within my heart and mind.

One way to slow down is to walk more slowly. This leading with your body is very powerful. It takes concentration to slow our walking, as we are always on our way to the next important place. But to rush to the next destination is to miss God in the present. You might also drive a little more slowly when it is in your power to do so and when traffic dictates. I have added eating more slowly, brushing my teeth longer, and adopting a slower pace in the morning. This slowing down helps me to become aware of my surroundings and what I am feeling internally. A good question to ask yourself as you seek to live more slowly is, "Am I currently feeling *driven* or *drawn* through life?" Driven-ness connotes a compulsive need for activity that comes from within. Drawn-ness speaks of an internal response to the invitation of another, a yielded-ness, a following, a responding-to.

SOLITUDE AND SILENCE

Solitude and silence are the fundamental disciplines involved in a life seeking to live Jesus. These twin disciplines afford us the greatest single opportunity to hear from God, to become aware of the ways God communicates with us, and to come to know God and self in ways that nurture a deeper desire for God.

Solitude, a foundational spiritual discipline, is something we see practiced by Jesus repeatedly, as he slipped away to be alone with his Father (Mark 6:46, Luke 4:42, 6:12). This discipline begins as an external reality, but it can, over time, become an internalized reality. You can develop the ability to pull within yourself in such a way that you and God are alone with one another even in the midst of a crowd of people. Dallas Willard says of solitude, "It is solitude and solitude alone that opens up the possibility of a radical relationship with God that can withstand all external events up to and beyond death."[3]

Solitude does not just happen; it involves a choice and intentional actions on our part, as the world seems to conspire against it. Thomas Merton reminds us, "You will never find interior solitude unless you make some conscious effort to deliver yourself from the desires and the cares and the attachments of an existence in time and in the world."[4] As you go through your day, intentionally notice the opportunities for solitude already built in—taking a shower, driving or walking by yourself, a lunch alone—and embrace them as opportunities to be intentionally with God. Present yourself—heart, mind, spirit—paying attention to the what and who of those moments, aware of and responsive to the way(s) God may communicate with you.

An experience of solitude can be difficult. You may feel naked and exposed, since there is no way to achieve a sense of worth from your words or your actions; no one is around to tell you how special or indispensable you are. In solitude we are who we are in Christ, nothing more, but more importantly, nothing less. Alone with God, we can begin to own who we truly are.

Silence is the ceasing from words and inward striving. It begins as an outward discipline, but the goal is that it would become an inward reality. As you begin to be silent, you will discover the tremendous amount of noise ("unsilence") that you carry with you in your heart and mind. The journey of silence *is a journey toward internal silence that will help you to hear the still small voice of God and to more readily be aware of what is stirring within you.*

Silence is often thought of as the absence of words or sounds, but it is more than that. It is the optimum environment for listening. If you want to have a serious conversation with someone, you find a quiet, even secluded, place. So even in our daily practice, there is this inherent knowing that silence fosters listening. Have you ever noticed that the same letters that spell silent, when rearranged, spell listen? Silence helps us attend and listen to God, to be aware of the Spirit of God, and to be aware of what the Spirit plants in our souls and what surfaces within our hearts.

In silence, extraneous things settle and clarity comes. You notice that noise can be a cover for sadness, anger, self-loathing, loneliness, despair—inner desolation that hinders your ability to recognize the inner promptings of the Spirit. But if you can stay with the feelings that you become aware of in silence, and invite God into those hidden places, you will begin to find healing. You will begin to hear God.

Insights for entering into silence:

1. *Dealing with internal noise:*

   Notice the messages lying just below the surface in your mind.
   Silence can provide an opportunity to identify the voices that hinder
   your ability to accept God's love, to fully receive your significance
   as God's child. Initially, silence can be painful, as you may be bat-

tered by negative voices within, but through God's transforming love your heart can be healed in silent communion with the One who loves you unconditionally.

2. *Dealing with troublesome thoughts in silence:*

Don't be shocked or even discouraged by your thoughts. God knew them before they came to your mind. If sin is revealed, confess it, allowing God time to show you the source and remind you of God's unconditional love, forgiveness, and grace.

3. *Be open to whatever God may bring your way:*

You may be led to a passage of scripture, invited to take a walk, to nap, sing, dance, discover something to explore or ponder (passage of scripture, attribute of God, decision, relationship). Let God take the lead as you pay attention to what is surfacing within. It can be a wonderful opportunity for journaling, but beware of distractions. Music, reading (even the Bible), and/or journaling can be an escape, a hindrance to silence and the self discovery God is leading you into.

Although solitude and silence can be practiced separately *the magnitude of their power is only fully experienced as they are fused together as a unit.*

One of my first experiences of the profound power of silence and solitude occurred near the end of my bicycle trip across the United States. As I bedded down for the

> "Solitude and inner silence provide the most promising environment for hearing the still small voice.[5]"
>
> —Marjorie J. Thompson

night inside a church at Red House, Maryland, alone in the quiet, God's message to me changed the course of my life. That night God made it clear that my bicycle trip, along with my grand plans to travel to Europe were now over. I was to return home and enroll in Bible school. That night a new path opened before me—a path I still walk.

HEART AWARENESS

As you practice the three S's of awareness—slowing down, solitude, and silence—you will become able to carry these realities with you. You can learn
to create and maintain an internal "sanctuary," regardless of the push and
shove of your circumstances, to develop an inner sensitivity to the voice of
God and the promptings of the Spirit in your heart. You might be tempted to
think of this heart communication solely in terms of emotions, but awareness
of the heart that leads to Christian discernment encompasses both feelings and
also a deep, transcendent knowing—a knowing that you know that you know.
It is similar to the burning of the heart spoken of in the gospels (Luke 24:32)
or the prayer of Paul that the eyes of the heart would be enlightened (Eph.
1:18). It is this developing *heart awareness* that enables you to more fully
align your heart with the heart of God. Heart awareness and the corresponding alignment of your heart with the heart of God is essential when it comes
to discernment and embodying God will.

Slowing, silence, and solitude enable you to become aware of your external circumstances, and to be present to the Presence within the present
moment both externally and also internally. When it comes to internal heart
awareness, there are two key terms to become familiar with: *consolation* and
desolation. Originally introduced by St. Ignatius of Loyola, these terms are
not precisely defined, but Ignatius offers two helpful characteristics. The first
focuses on the affect: consolations are interior movements in the soul generated by an inflamed love for God. A consolation can result from sorrow for
one's sins, passion for Christ, increased hope, faith, love, or joy. Desolations
involve all that is contrary to consolations, such as darkness of the soul, internal uneasiness, agitations and temptations, hopelessness, and so on. The
focus of these definitions is on your interior feelings. God does make use of
our feelings.

However Ignatius also speaks of volitional consolation and/or desolation,
which changes the emphasis from feelings and instead focuses on where a circumstance, internal feeling, interaction, etc. is taking us: toward God or away

from God. Thus volitional consolation is defined as an interior movement toward God and volitional desolation infers interior movement away from God—regardless of your feelings of pain or peace, comfort or confusion, joy or sadness. The best way to think about volitional consolation and desolation is in terms of an individual's inner orientation. *The key question is not, What am I feeling? (though this still remains an important question), but, Which direction is my life (emotions, circumstances, interactions, thoughts, etc.) taking me? Toward God or away from God?*

As you learn to be aware of, sensitive and responsive to, the inner moments of your spirit toward to or away from God, you will be prepared for an even deeper, more profound—yet subtle—internal heart awareness that will be key to discerning/decision-making. This topic will be discussed later (see Section Four), but I share it here to stress the importance of the cultivation of the three S's of awareness and the corresponding development of your ability to be aware of your internal feelings of consolation and desolation. Volitional consolation and desolation are critical components when it comes to embodying God's will and living Jesus.

Below are a list of characteristics of affective and/or volitional desolation. As you become familiar with these characteristics, you will more readily realize when you have turned away from God and can choose to reorient your life.

Affective and/or Volitional Desolation:

- Turns us in on ourselves
- Drives us down the spiral ever deeper into our own negative feelings
- Cuts us off from community
- Makes things that used to be important to us seem to have no value to us
- Takes over our whole consciousness and limits our vision; we become myopic
- Covers up all our landmarks of God's past grace and goodness

- Drains us of energy to be proactive

- Takes us into places of feeling helpless and hopeless

- Makes us focus on the temporal—things one can taste, see, touch….

- Can be an indictor of a disordered attachment (i.e., we are not indifferent)

(Margaret Silf)[6]

The goal of slowing down, solitude, and silence is to develop an internal heart awareness that enables you to be in tune with the internal prompting of the Spirit, and your inner movements toward God or away from God, so that you will have the internal space to turn aside from the demands and responsibilities of the moment, as Moses did with the burning bush, and come to know and embody God's will in the midst of living your life each day.

> *A discernment principle associated with consolation and desolation is as follows: Do not change a decision made during a time of consolation when you are in a time of desolation. This is very helpful, yet many of the decisions that are made are made during times of desolation.*

EXERCISES:

1. *As you move through your day, try to incorporate the three S's of awareness:*

a. slow down

- *Be open (seek to be in the now of your day, present to the One who is present to you, present within you).*
- *Walk slowly (take your time, do not rush but slow down, be aware of and attentive to that around you and stirring within you).*
- *Bow often (allow yourself to be surprised by God, to be captured by the moment and then turn aside and drink in the gift you are experiencing, allowing wonder, gratitude, and thanksgiving to well up within you).*

b. solitude

- *Be attentive during those times you are alone; taking a shower, driving alone somewhere, going for a walk, sitting in a park, getting up early in the morning. It is often quite easy to pair solitude with silence.*

c. silence

- *Turn off the noise when you drive, get ready in the morning, or take a break, so that you can listen to the God who often speaks in and out of the silence. Gradually become aware of those internal voices that lead you away from God, that hinder you from following God, that lie to you regarding your worth, value, and significance. Replace them with the truths of whose you are and who you are.*
- *Set aside ten minutes of silence. What do you hear, externally, internally? Let all the noise go and begin to be present to God beyond words. Use a timer so you are not continually checking the clock.*

- *Begin your prayer time in silence. Let go of the internal racket in order to be fully present to God as you pray and read the scriptures.*

2. *Ask God to help you briefly review your day, recalling to mind interactions throughout your day and asking the question, "Was I internally feeling the affect of consolation or desolation? Was my heart moving toward God, in alignment with God's heart (volitional consolation), or moving away from God (volitional desolation)?" This prayer practice is designed to help you foster internal awareness. It is not about generating condemnation, but recognizing what is going on within you.*

3. *Take a contemplative walk, walking slowly, deliberately. Use all your five senses as you walk. Start by being aware of the light, the warmth of the sun, the touch of the air, and the colors around you. Then begin to notice greater detail in patterns, shapes, textures, the shades of colors, the contrasts and juxtapositions and how natural things relate. Touch and feel, pick up stones, twigs, earth, leaves, and hold them gently. Try to stop thinking and simply to be. Let everything drop away and try to be totally present to what is reaching you through your senses. Begin to notice smell more acutely, the scent of growing things, of the earth itself. Listen to the range of sounds, far-off distant sounds, those that are close, your own breathing. You may want to bring back a memento, something that you particularly enjoyed. End with a thanksgiving exercise, consciously listing the discoveries God has given you during your walk and thanking God for all.*

SECTION THREE: BIBLICAL FOUNDATIONS

This section is the foundation for all that is in this book. In addition to presenting two ways to look at and understand God's will, we will explore the critical roles that the Holy Spirit and the scriptures play in Christian discernment. There is no Christian discernment possible apart from the ministry of the Holy Spirit and the living and active word of God.

As you were encouraged to do in section one, please pay attention to those things you are drawn to and resistant toward. Continue to see resistance as an invitation to turn aside and pay attention, to reflect on, and then to respond to what you discover. This recognizing, reflecting on, and responding to are key components of the process of Christian discernment. So, as you recognize and pay attention to what you are drawn to and resistant toward, you are training yourself to become a discerning person.

CHAPTER SEVEN

THE WILL OF GOD

In my early days as a Christian, the topic of God's will was very popular. Books on the subject abounded and Christians of all ages turned to them for advice or enlightenment. The desire to know and follow God's will for one's life ran deep—and still generates a lively discussion. At some point the focus shifted from finding God's will for one's life to asking the question, "What would Jesus do (WWJD)?" The idea was that, when faced with a decision, you would pause and first ask, WWJD?

This shift of focus brought with it a welcome emphasis on living out God's will, but it was predicated on the hubris of believing you could, with some level of certainty, answer the question, "What would Jesus do?" And so WWJD became a vehicle for promoting individual theologies. I remember an individual using WWJD to explain his decision to buy a car with good gas mileage as opposed to a gas-guzzling SUV—for him it was easy to know what Jesus would do. The truth is that at any given moment we do not know what Jesus is going to do. The disciples ran into this time and time again as they endeavored to anticipate Jesus' next move or even to understand the reasons behind the things he did.

Would Jesus buy a hybrid, an SUV, an electric car? Would Jesus ever be in the 15-items-or-less line at the grocery store, knowing he had 17 items? Would Jesus meet alone with a woman? Would Jesus vote Democratic or Republican? Your answer to any of these questions speaks more about you than it does about Jesus. The truth is that in the concrete realities of daily life, we do not know what Jesus would do other than this: Jesus would do as the Father told him to do, as the Spirit led him.

More recently, the Christian community has moved beyond God's will and WWJD, and on to the topic of discernment. "Discernment" is now the common term employed when one speaks of desiring to follow Jesus, to live out God's will. As stated earlier, discernment involves distinguishing among all the possibilities, all the inner stirrings, thoughts, voices, and impulses, in order to determine what path to take or decision to make. Yet the question remains, what is meant by God's will and how can we know it?

The words of Jesus and Paul both convey the importance of knowing God's will. In the prayer Jesus teaches his disciples, the pivotal petition is a request that God's kingdom come and God's will be done. When Jesus speaks about the importance of the will of God in his own life, he likens it to food—it sustains him. Paul writes to the church of Ephesus concerning God's will, "Therefore do not be foolish, but understand what the will of the Lord is" (Eph. 5:17) and he also writes about "doing the will of God from the heart" (6:6b). He prays for those in Colossae, "asking that [they] may be filled with the knowledge of [God's] will in all spiritual wisdom and understanding..." (Col. 1:9b), and to the Romans he writes, "Do not be conformed to this world, but be transformed by the renewal of your mind, that by testing you may discern what is the will of God, what is good and acceptable and perfect" (Rom. 12:2). For Jesus and Paul, God's will being done on earth and in heaven was of supreme importance.

So, what is meant by "God's will"? The answer is not as straightforward as it may seem. When it comes to God's will, there are a number of misunderstandings, partial truths and oversimplifications that can hinder our ability to determine God's will. There certainly is not a consensus—in fact the subject produces more questions than answers. Does God have a perfect will for an individual's life? Is the Bible the full embodiment of God's will, serving as a textbook for life? Does God have an individual will for each person? Is God's will a bullseye we must hit each and every time we make a decision? There isn't space to deal with each of these fully, but I will briefly comment on them and then present two images that describe what I believe to be God's will.

GOD'S PERFECT WILL

Many seem to feel that God has a perfect will, God's Plan A, for each of us, and it is our responsibility to discover and follow that plan. Often those who are sincerely seeking this perfect plan of God's carry a foreboding that they will miss it, or have missed it and must settle for a life that is less than what God intended. They may be discouraged, even convinced they are no longer able to serve God. The truth is that Plan A is no longer available to any of us! Adam and Eve blew that out of the water millenniums ago. If you are one of those Plan A people who believe you've missed the boat and had to settle for less than God wanted for you, join the crowd named humanity. The good news is you are still able to experience the abundant life that Jesus made available through his death and resurrection. You are able to live Jesus, to embody God's will, even though there is no perfect plan this side of heaven.

THE BIBLE ALONE

Another perspective on God's will is the Bible textbook view: that the Bible is all we need to live God's will. Unlike the "Plan A" view (which is totally incorrect), this opinion is partially true. The Bible does clearly communicate how humanity is to live: it gives us the Ten Commandments, the two great commandments (love God and love others), Paul's admonitions regarding how to live and how to interact with others within and outside the faith, and the list goes on. According to some, God's will is fully revealed and completely spelled out in the Bible, available to all who follow it.

Part of the emphasis on the Bible alone as the sole declaration of God's will is due to a desire to remove the mystical, supernatural, and transcendent components of Christian discernment, to reduce it to following the concrete truths as revealed in scripture. One writer/speaker who adopts this view lists six things that the Bible says are God's will for us. He says if you make these things a part of your life, you can do whatever you want. This certainly takes the mystery out of embodying God's will, BUT it is not the way Jesus lived his life. To live Jesus, while ordering one's life in accordance with scripture, entails much more than merely reading the Bible and doing what it says. It involves components that are mysterious, supernatural, relational, and transcendent—qualities which don't necessarily make the process difficult, but definitely more involved than simply reading the Bible.

Before moving on, I want to make it clear that the Bible plays a very important role in Christian discernment. But it does not play the only role, nor does it play the most important role. This may cause a bit of unease, but will be clarified in the next two chapters. For now, let's look at two images that convey helpful truths about the nature of God's will.

THE MEADOW

The first image of God's will is that of a large, spacious meadow in which we are free to live our lives. Although the meadow is quite expansive, it is still a contained space. There is a permeable boundary that circles the entire meadow, the fence of God's word. As long as we are in the meadow, we are free to romp, dance, serve, create—to live an abundant life. There is great freedom within the meadow, freedom to be and to become, to journey with others, to grow in the realization of God's love and in our ability to love and serve others. It is important to note that the meadow in not a protective bubble, nor are there only Christians in this meadow. The meadow has its share of challenges, as the boundary of God's word, while helpful, does not keep us from transgressing. Nor does it keep the other stuff of life out. There will be struggles, suffering, and temptations alongside the joy and freedom the meadow provides. God's will as a meadow speaks to a freedom to live one's life, but it is not a freedom of autonomy. It is a freedom born out of and maintained through relationship with the Good Shepherd, a life lived listening for and willing to follow the Shepherd's voice, a life yielded to and dependent on the Shepherd (John 10).

THE BULLSEYE

The second image of God's will is a bullseye, a precise target, which may be hard to reconcile with the expanse of the meadow, but the meadow and bullseye are not mutually exclusive. There are times when you are frolicking in the meadow without a care in the world, and you hear the Shepherd saying that it's time to move to another area in the meadow, possibly one that is not as lush or as close to a water source. In times like these, the meadow is transformed into a bullseye, and your freedom to playfully move about is taken from you, as God makes God's bullseye will known.

This new place, since it is in the meadow, still offers freedom and is still a place to experience joy, but experiencing that joy may take time. For now, the spaciousness of the meadow has been greatly reduced, and the ongoing invitation of freedom has been replaced by the challenge of particular obedience. The choice remains yours. This is when you experience firsthand the importance of the truth conveyed in the second section of this book: you need to know whose you are (God is for you, with you, loving you), who you are (loved by God, chosen, belonging to God), and you must be indifferent, free from disordered attachments that would hinder your ability to say yes to God. There is joy to be had in the bullseye—in fact it is often a gateway to a deeper experience of the abundant life in Christ. It is an invitation to greater growth in the image of Christ, toward becoming the person God created and called you to be.

This movement from the spaciousness of the meadow to the felt confines of the bullseye is not easily navigated. It brings with it, at least initially, its own challenges, but over time the bullseye opens up and becomes a meadow of sorts. You experience freedom once again. I've experienced this numerous times in my own life. I had been enjoying the freedom of the meadow when suddenly the Shepherd communicated a change of plans, a move, a career change, a reduction in salary, a loss of community and even, once, the loss of our home. We were led to leave the lush meadow for a place where the grass was sparse, and I was not sure if it could sustain our family of six. There was great pain early on, but after a couple of years there, the grass started to grow and our family began to enjoy this new place. We were not merely sustained; we flourished. As I look back on that decade, I recall the great joy and freedom experienced while becoming more of who God had created and called me to be. The bullseye of change stretched and I roamed a wondrous meadow of God's will once again.

God's will is both vast like a meadow and at times very

> *Too often it is assumed that God's will, bullseye or meadow, is always contrary to our desires, always involves taking the most difficult and demanding path. This is NOT true. God also leads us into green meadows and alongside quiet waters. Beware of automatically assuming that the difficult, the thing that you would most hate doing, is what God wants you to do—it is not always the case and I believe it is not even mostly the case.*

exacting like hitting a bullseye, and both realities coexist. God is with us, loving us, and empowering us, because the Good Shepherd does not change and his will for us is a hope and a future.

You have probably guessed by now that I *do* believe God has an individual will for our lives—not a "Plan A" type of will, but one that is true to who we have been created and called to be. Paul tells us in Ephesians 2:10, "For we are his workmanship, created in Christ Jesus for good works, which God prepared beforehand, that we should walk in them." This idea of an individual will is seen in the lives of many followers of God in both the Old and New Testaments.

INDIVIDUAL WILL

Many Christians believe God doesn't get involved in individual will. Instead, they believe that God has expressed God's will for us in the scriptures, and that to do God's will is a matter of applying biblical truths to the circumstances of our lives, using wisdom and reason. They acknowledge that God did individually lead some people, but those individuals were exceptions to the way God works, and are relegated to a certain period of time, generally before the indwelling of the Spirit and certainly before the completion of the Bible. The argument is that since we now have the completed scriptures that reveal to us God's moral will, we are no longer in need of God's direct leading. This line of thinking tracks with the idea of the Bible as the sole repository of God's will for humanity, as we've already touched on.

The major sticking point for those who come out against God having an individual will for people is the subjective nature involved in discerning God's individual will. They argue that dependence on hearing from God, being led by the inner promptings of the Holy Spirit, provides no objective source by which one can determine with certainty that they can know God's individual will, and that this dependence actually promotes immaturity by permitting believers to justify unwise decisions on the grounds, "God told me to do it." I would argue to the contrary. Recorded in both old and new testaments, this individual will of God actually fosters the need for a deepening of one's relationship with God, of having a relationship with God characterized by listening and awareness. Such depth is seen most convincingly in the relationship Jesus had with the Father, a mature relationship characterized not by independence, but by greater dependence on God (see Chapter 16, "Adult Faith").

One scholar who writes against individual will, Garry Freisen, defines it as follows: "[The] individual will is that ideal, detailed life-plan which God has uniquely designed for each believer. This life-plan encompasses every decision we make and is the basis of God's daily guidance. This guidance is given through the indwelling of the Holy Spirit who progressively reveals God's life-plan to the heart of the individual believer."[1]

Freisen is largely fair in his definition of individual will. As a believer in individual will, I do believe that guidance is given through the indwelling of the Holy Spirit who communicates to the heart of the believer, a guidance that is uniquely designed by God for that person, and that these communications are given to help the individual to make God-honoring life choices. However, when Freisen writes of the individual will as a detailed life-plan that accompanies every decision we make, I think he is setting up a bit of a straw-man. His definition becomes too expansive (every decision) and too precise (detailed life-plan).

Going back to the image of the meadow: I believe there are times, quite possibly more times than we realize, when God invites us to a particular place within the meadow *and this is what I refer to as God's individual will*. It is a will communicated to us by God through the Holy Spirit, uniquely in harmony with who we are and who God created us to be. God's will can be a meadow or a bullseye.

I want to conclude this chapter with Dallas Willard's comments regarding those individuals who do not see or have a place for the personal guidance of God in the lives of individuals:

"It seems to me that one of the most damaging things we can do to the spiritual prospects of anyone is to suggest to or teach that God will not deal with them specifically, personally, intelligibly, and consciously or that they cannot count on him to do so as he sees fit. Once we have conveyed this idea to them, it makes no sense to attempt to lead them into an honestly personal relationship with God.[2]"

Note: The bottom line of God's will is love God and love others. If that is true of your life—whether you are in the meadow or the bullseye or not quite sure where you are—God is pleased!

EXERCISES:

1. *If you do see an individual will of God, do you view it more as a meadow where you are generally free to roam, or as a bullseye you had better hit? Why?*

2. *Do you believe God still uniquely guides and directs us, or is the Bible all we need to live a God-honoring life each day? Why or why not?*

3. *Have you experienced the personal guidance of God? If yes, how did you know it was God? What was it like to hear from God in a personal way? When is the last time you had a sense of God leading you? If no, why do you think that is?*

CHAPTER EIGHT

THE ROLE OF THE HOLY SPIRIT

N ow we turn our attention to the single most important player in Christian discernment: the Holy Spirit. Our definition of Christian discernment points to the critical empowerment of the Spirit; it is that empowerment that enables us to recognize the communications of God, distinguish good from evil, perceive what is best, and embody God's will. But many Christians are at a loss when it comes to turning to the Holy Spirit as the agent of discernment. Francis Chan refers to the Holy Spirit as "the forgotten God."

In my own early church experience, we spoke about the Trinity but the focus was on the Father and the Son. I got the sense that the Holy Spirit was like a distant relative you mention from time to time but never invite to any family gatherings, not sure of how he'd behave. I had heard stories of the wild happenings in those places where the Spirit was invited and welcome—selective stories with the implicit message that one is to keep one's distance. So I did.

This suspicious, distrustful attitude regarding the Spirit impedes spiritual growth and tends to cultivate a dependence on external authority figures, failing to take both the words of Jesus and his example seriously. One important element of the Christian life that is particularly affected by lack of intimacy with the Holy Spirit is Christian discernment. I'm not saying Christians cannot make God-honoring decisions without depending on the Spirit; God is gracious, and even a blind squirrel finds a nut occasionally. But it is not, as they say, best practice.

Christian discernment has largely become discernment devoid of the Spirit and dependent solely on an intellectual process, employing reason, scripture, common sense, and pros and cons for decision making. God may be called in to begin the discernment process and, once the decision is arrived at, invited to confirm and bless the decision, but God is not included as a real participant. The resulting process may be comfortable and make intellectual sense, but is Spiritless.

> *The Holy Spirit is to be the most real and powerful factor in our daily lives. We need to walk throughout the day in a relationship of communication and communion with the Spirit mediated through our knowledge of the word, relying upon every office of the Holy Spirit's role as counselor mentioned in scripture. We need to see the Spirit as illuminator of truth and of the glory of Christ. Looking to the Spirit as teacher, guide, sanctifier, giver of assurance concerning our Sonship and standing before God, helper in prayer, and as the one who directs and empowers witness.*
>
> –Richard F. Lovelace[1]

It is time to put our fears and prejudices (I admit I was Spirit-phobic) aside and recapture the New Testament's view of the predominate role the Holy Spirit plays in the lives of those who know and are seeking to live Jesus, practice Christian discernment, and embody God's will. We ignore the ministry of the Spirit in our lives at our own peril. Paul even warns us, *"Do not quench the Spirit (emphasis mine)"* (1 Thess. 5:19) and *"do not grieve the Holy Spirit of God (emphasis mine)"* (Eph. 4:30). I fear when it comes to the current practices of discernment, we are both quenching AND grieving the Holy Spirit. We need to recover the New Testament sense of the role of the

Holy Spirit in the Christian life. It is the Holy Spirit that guides and directs us whether in the vast meadow or the bullseye of God's will.

JESUS' WORDS ABOUT THE HOLY SPIRIT

In John 16:7, Jesus makes an astonishing assertion regarding his view of his subsequent departure and the arrival of the Helper (the Holy Spirit):

> *Nevertheless, I tell you the truth: it is to your advantage ["for your good" (NIV), "best for you" (NLT)] that I go away, for if I do not go away, the Helper will not come to you. But if I go, I will send him to you.*

These are not Jesus' only words regarding the Holy Spirit (also referred to as Advocate, Counselor, Spirit of Truth, Comforter, Helper, to name a few) but they are clear about Jesus' opinion of the value of the Spirit. Let Jesus' words sink in for a few moments. He is telling his disciples that it is BETTER that he is no longer physically present with them so that the Holy Spirit will come. This new arrangement, the coming and indwelling of the Spirit, will be exceedingly beneficial for them.

In and around this passage, Jesus provides a laundry list of what the Spirit will do: testify to the world about sin, righteousness, and judgment (John 16:8); teach and remind Jesus' followers of everything he has said to them, testify about Jesus (John 14:26); guide them into truth, not speak on his own; speak only what he hears, and tell them what is yet to come…the Spirit will receive from Jesus what he will make known to them (John 16:12–15). The bottom line is that the gift of the Holy Spirit is an upgrade from the physical presence of Jesus, making the words of the Father and the Son available to us as never before.

PAUL'S WORDS ABOUT THE HOLY SPIRIT

The Apostle Paul expands on Jesus' list of the benefits of the coming and indwelling of the Holy Spirit. Paul writes that the Spirit leads us, testifies that we are children of God, prays for us, helps us to understand what God has freely given us, teaches us, confirms that Jesus lives within us, transforms us, brings freedom, seals us for the day of redemption, sanctifies us, fills our hearts with God's love, gives us spiritual gifts, strengthens us with power, enables Jesus' presence to be in us, and gives us wisdom and understanding. Paul also encourages us to be filled with the Spirit, to pray and love in the Spirit, and to walk by the Spirit. For Paul, being led by the Spirit is the ultimate apologetic regarding a person's identity as a child of God. (Romans 8:14: "For those who are led by the Spirit of God are the children of God." (NIV))

This experience of being led by the Spirit is reminiscent of Jesus' life. At the very beginning of his ministry, following the baptism, the scripture says, "Then Jesus was led up by the Spirit into the wilderness" (Matt. 4:1a). The Spirit led Jesus and now we too can be—and are expected to be—led by the Spirit, as this is a hallmark of Christian identity. Over and over again, Paul tells us to be filled by the Spirit, live by the Spirit, walk by the Spirit, pray in the Spirit, love in the Spirit. Paul cannot envision living Jesus, embodying God's will, apart from a Spirit-empowered and infused life.

DISCERNMENT, THE HOLY SPIRIT AND THE EARLY CHURCH

Luke writes in Acts of the dramatic appearance of the Spirit that marks the beginning of the Church (Acts 2:1–13). Jesus is no longer physically present and the promised era of the coming, indwelling and empowering of the Spirit begins. In this remarkable incident, the possibility of Christian discernment is also born. As Luke records the unfolding history of the Church in Acts, we see the important role the Spirit plays for those early believers seeking to embody God's will (emphasis mine in all cases):

- Act 15:28: "For it has seemed *good to the Holy Spirit and to us* to lay on you no greater burden than these requirements..."
- Acts 13:2: "While they were worshiping the Lord and fasting, *the Holy Spirit said*, 'Set apart for me Barnabas and Saul for the work to which I have called them.'"

- Acts 16:6–7: "And they went through the region of Phrygia and Galatia, *having been forbidden by the Holy Spirit to speak the word* in Asia. And when they had come up to Mysia, they attempted to go into Bithynia, *but the Spirit of Jesus did not allow them.*"

- Acts 16:9–10: "And *a vision appeared to Paul* in the night: a man of Macedonia was standing there, urging him and saying, 'Come over to Macedonia and help us.' And when Paul[a] had seen the vision, immediately we sought to go on into Macedonia, *concluding that God had called* us to preach the gospel to them."

- Acts 18:9: And *the Lord said to Paul one night in a vision*, 'Do not be afraid, but go on speaking and do not be silent…'"

Those in the early church depended on the Spirit to lead and guide them as they sought to follow Christ. The above passages tell us that the Holy Spirit communicates in a variety of ways. The Spirit directs us regarding what to do and what not to do, so it becomes imperative, as Jesus said, to have ears to hear (be aware). John also, in the concluding book of the Bible, urges the people, "Whoever has ears, let them hear what the Spirit says to the churches" (Rev. 2:11, NIV). Thus, it is important to develop the ability to hear what the Spirit is saying.

HOLY SPIRIT AND GOD'S WORD

One way we begin to hear and distinguish the communications of the Spirit is to spend time reading, studying and pondering the scriptures. The Holy Spirit will never contradict the words of scripture. Slowly read the following passage, paying attention to the role of the Holy Spirit when it comes to understanding the truths, thoughts, and words of God communicated in and through the scriptures.

> None of the rulers of this age understood this, for if they had, they would not have crucified the Lord of glory. But, as it is written,
>
> "What no eye has seen, nor ear heard, nor the heart of man imagined, what God has prepared for those who love him"–these things God has

revealed to us through the Spirit. For the Spirit searches everything, even the depths of God. For who knows a person's thoughts except the spirit of that person, which is in him? So also no one comprehends the thoughts of God except the Spirit of God. Now we have received not the spirit of the world, but the Spirit who is from God, that we might understand the things freely given us by God. And we impart this in words not taught by human wisdom but taught by the Spirit, interpreting spiritual truths to those who are spiritual.

The natural person does not accept the things of the Spirit of God, for they are folly to him, and he is not able to understand them because they are spiritually discerned. The spiritual person judges all things, but is himself to be judged by no one. "For who has understood the mind of the Lord so as to instruct him?" But we have the mind of Christ. (1 Cor. 2:8–16)

A brief exploration of this amazing passage reveals that the Holy Spirit makes available to us things beyond our natural ability to understand. The Spirit communicates and helps us understand the deep things of God freely given by God. The Holy Spirit, using spiritual words, teaches us important spiritual truths and animates the mind of Christ within us. Through the indwelling of the Spirit, we have access to the thoughts of God and are privy to the deeper spiritual realities of life and of the heart of God.

In a manner never possible before the gift of the Spirit, the thoughts and ways of God can be our thoughts and our ways. As Jesus tells us, we are now his friends and, through the indwelling of the Spirit, we are let in on what God is up to. We now have the possibility and responsibility to learn and listen to the Spirit and to cultivate the mind of Christ in order to embody God's will.

CHOOSING THE BEST

The presence of the Spirit gives us the capacity to grow beyond merely choosing between good and evil (Heb. 5:12–14); we can now develop the ability to discern what is best. Paul writes, "And this is my prayer: that your love may abound more and more in knowledge and depth of insight, so that you may be *able to discern what is best...*" (Phil 1:9–10a NIV emphasis mine). The Greek words used in the passage imply a spiritual aspect to the knowledge and insight Paul desires for his readers. This spiritual knowledge and insight is only possible with the help of the Holy Spirit.

Perceiving what is best is extremely important when it comes to Christian discernment. As we grow in our faith and are not as easily tempted by the things that are overtly evil, Satan changes his strategy and begins to appear as an Angel of Light. Satan is now willing to lead us into pursuits that, while good, will intentionally prevent us from God's BEST (more about this in Chapter 12). The gift of Christian discernment, when cultivated by developing a deeper knowledge of God and self and incorporating an awareness of the promptings of the Spirit, helps us choose those things which are not merely allowable (lawful), but are profitable, beneficial, and constructive (1 Cor. 6:12, 10:23), while holy indifference frees us to choose what is best.

BACK TO EDEN

The coming of the Spirit has radically changed the dynamic of our relationship with God. We now have the opportunity to walk with God, hear from God, and speak with God with a relational intimacy that is akin to a return to the Garden of Eden. This shared life with God is depicted in a number of ways: father/child, friends, lovers, husband/wife, each portraying various levels of relational intimacy. This life the Holy Spirit makes available to us is very different than the life that flows from the sin of Adam—that was an independent life where one determines good from evil apart from God. Now, with the coming of the Spirit, the original order has been restored and the independence resulting from the fall is replaced by a relational dependence on the wisdom and insight of God.

The coming and indwelling of the Holy Spirit changes everything. It is no wonder Jesus was so unwavering about the importance of the Spirit. The words of Jesus and Paul emphasize the predominance of the Holy Spirit when it comes to living the Christian life and practicing Christian discernment. We are expected to walk and be led by the Spirit—a life of relational connection with God. As we walk in the Spirit, we receive the wisdom that comes from above and the scriptures are opened to us in new and deeper ways; cultivating the mind of Christ within us and enabling us to choose that which is best.

EXERCISES:

Intentionally invite God into your decision-making process and prayer life this week, and as you do, endeavor to be indifferent to all else, except to choose God's best in love, honor, and service.

1. In little decisions—which line to stand in at the store, where to sit at Church, whether or not to watch TV, to go online—ask God to guide you and then act on what you sense God may be saying, how God may be leading you.

2. When you pray for people, ask God how to pray for them; be open to the Spirit leading you to write a note, send a text, email. Don't assume you know what to pray for or even that the person knows what they truly need; let God guide and direct your prayers.

3. Endeavor to continue to be aware of those spontaneous thoughts, impulses, and promptings that arise within you, not quickly dismissing or discounting them, but be open to them as possibly coming from God via the Holy Spirit. See where they take you, remembering that, if they are from God, they will never lead you in ways that are contrary to scripture.

DAILY PRACTICE:

This week, begin to pray the Prayer of Awareness at least once a day until you finish the book. You will find this prayer in the appendix. This prayer cultivates an internal awareness of the Spirit and keeps you connected to God throughout your day. The video for this chapter will walk you through the steps of this prayer and provide tips to help make it part of your life. Go to www.b-ing.org and click on Christian Discernment. Pray this prayer in addition to the Prayer of Recollection.

CHAPTER NINE

THE ROLE OF SCRIPTURE

This chapter is grounded in the simple truth that the scriptures are alive, and you are not so much invited to read the scriptures as you are to encounter and interact with God *through* the scriptures.

Two passages in particular communicate the vitality and the life (aliveness) of the biblical text. The first is found in 2 Timothy 3:16: "All Scripture is breathed out by God..." This passage is often the mighty club wielded in the defense of biblical inerrancy, but that is not our debate today. Our focus is on the uniqueness of scripture. In Genesis we discover that it is the breath of God that gives life to mankind and so it is with the scriptures. They are God-breathed—they are alive. It is this "God-breathed" component that makes the Bible different from any other writing in history

The second passage is found in Hebrews 4:12 and is more straightforward: "For the word of God is living and active, sharper than any two-edged sword, piercing to the division of soul and of spirit, of joints and of marrow, and discerning the thoughts and intentions of the heart." This passage argues that indeed scripture is alive, and as a living thing, it is dynamic and active. Isaiah 55:11 also comments on the active component of God's word:

"So shall my word be that goes out from my mouth; it shall not return to me empty, but it shall accomplish that which I purpose, and shall succeed in the thing for which I sent it." Thus it comes as no surprise that Paul encourages the followers of Jesus to let the word of Christ richly dwell within them.

The living word of God is key to living God's will, so our focus in this chapter is on meditation and study, hearing and learning God's living word with ears and hearts tuned to what the Spirit is teaching. Paul writes, "… no one comprehends the thoughts of God except the Spirit of God. Now we have received not the spirit of the world, but the Spirit who is from God, that we might understand the things freely given us by God. And we impart this in words not taught by human wisdom but taught by the Spirit, interpreting spiritual truths to those who are spiritual." (1 Cor 2:11b–13). Meditating on scripture and studying scripture help us to develop ears to hear what the Spirit is saying; truth that forms our hearts and shapes our desires.

Richard Foster says, "Although meditation and study often overlap and function concurrently, they constitute two distinct experiences. Study provides a certain objective framework within which meditation can successfully function."[1] Bible study involves engaging the mind on scripture to understand and apply truth to living. "Do not be conformed to this world, but be transformed by the renewal of your mind, that by testing you may discern what is the will of God, what is good and acceptable and perfect" (Rom 12:2).

Gordon T. Smith commented on the link between study, the Spirit, and discernment, pointing out that, "We cannot develop our intuitive capacity to recognize the inner witness unless we are women and men who are immersed in Scripture so that the contours of our hearts and minds are ordered and enabled by the Word."[2]

Both Bible study and meditation are important to living a life of Christian discernment. And while these two practices need to be considered together, I want to devote the remainder of this chapter to fostering the practice of meditation, focusing on three approaches to scripture reading/meditation that will help you open your heart and mind to the Holy Spirit. It is the Spirit who

translates God's words from another time and place and repeats them uniquely to us in ways that bring revelation, understanding, and even transformation. By engaging in these practices, reading scripture becomes more about
listening and opening to God and discovering a place of encounter, renewal,
challenge, and invitation.

These methods of interaction with scripture foster a deepening relationship with God by encouraging us to listen attentively to the words and the
promptings of the Spirit. In this case, we aren't looking for objective truth,
but rather an opening to the subjective, the felt reality of God through our
emotions—what we are feeling and sensing in our hearts. Although our emotions are not foundations upon which to build, they are windows to deeper
discoveries concerning God and self, and must not be ignored. This type of
heart-knowing is a change from the tendency to overemphasize propositional
truth. It is more than knowledge; it's a byproduct of personal engagement,
it is like the intimacy between husband and wife. These ways of interacting
with scripture are meant to foster an encounter with God, a knowing, a direct
experience of God in the heart.

OPEN TO GOD BY SLOWING DOWN

In this case, "slowing down" refers specifically to an act of personal prepara-
tion before entering into your daily time with God. It's a practice for readying
your heart, mind, and spirit to come before God. I'm suggesting two methods,
which each share a few common elements: breathing (focus on body), letting
go of thoughts, worries, pressures (focus on mind, heart), and prayer (focus
moves from self to God). These methods will help prepare you to be open to
what God has for you.

Exercise: Slow-down #1

Start by getting into a comfortable position. Once settled, begin to take slow, deep breaths, taking in enough air to expand your chest. Breathe in through your nose and out through your mouth. As you continue breathing, allow your mind to slow down, to let go of thoughts and worries. Release any tension in your body, continuing to take deep breaths in through your nose and out through your mouth. Imagine that God is breathing life, love, and peace into you with each breath you take in. As you breathe out, imagine stress, anxiety, fear, and burdens leaving you. Feel yourself sinking deeper and deeper into the presence of God.

Allow at least 3–5 minutes for this exercise before concluding with a silent prayer, offering yourself to God and asking for guidance through your time in the Word.

Exercise: Slow-down #2

Start by getting into a comfortable position. Once settled, begin to take slow, deep breaths, taking in enough air to expand your chest. Breathe in through your nose and out through your mouth. As you continue breathing, allow your mind to slow down, to let go of thoughts and worries. Release any tension in your body, continuing to take deep breaths in through your nose and out through your mouth. As you continue to slowly and deeply breathe, turn your hands over, palms down. Imagine yourself dropping those things that are weighing you down: worries, concerns, and frustrations, the things that bring you emotional discomfort or pain. When you feel you've been able to let them go, turn your hands palms up, representing your readiness to enter into imaginative prayer and receive what God has for you.

Allow at least 3-5 minutes for this exercise before concluding with a silent prayer, offering yourself to God and asking for guidance through your time in the Word.

MEDITATION

Meditation gets a bad rap as a spiritual discipline, although Christians and Jews have practiced it for centuries. Often it's associated with eastern religion and thus viewed with great suspicion, labeled as evil or even summarily dismissed. Yet meditation, mentioned often in the Psalms, is not only encouraged but is a powerful spiritual practice giving wisdom, inner strength, and power to participants. J. I. Packer says that "meditation is a lost art today. Christians suffer grievously from their ignorance of this practice."[3]

The type of meditation we are speaking of has its roots in the Hebrew faith. It provides the opportunity to ponder, sit with, explore, and internalize God's truth, encounter the person of God, expand one's heart, and refine one's desires. It involves giving attention to the moving and promptings of the Holy Spirit and it expands our ability to live a discerning life.

- "This Book of the Law shall not depart from your mouth, but you shall meditate on it day and night, so that you may be careful to do according to all that is written in it. For then you will make your way prosperous, and then you will have good success." –Joshua 1:8
- "...but his delight is in the law of the Lord, and on his law he meditates day and night." –Psalm 1:2
- "...when I remember you upon my bed, and meditate on you in the watches of the night..." –Psalm 63:6
- "I will ponder all your work, and meditate on your mighty deeds." –Psalms 77:12
- "My eyes are awake before the watches of the night, that I may meditate on your promise." –Psalm 119:148
- "I remember the days of old; I meditate on all that you have done; I ponder the work of your hands." –Psalm 143:5

The goal of meditation is to give the Holy Spirit the opportunity to guide us into transforming truth while fostering a spiritual perception that enlightens the eyes of our hearts. It involves deep and repetitive pondering of its subject. I think the word that best describes the mysterious inner workings of the meditative process is "ruminate"—to chew the cud like a cow. It's not a pretty picture, but it's an accurate one, as it refers to the way some animals chew and chew and chew their food, then swallow, regurgitate, and chew some more. By this slow, repetitive process, they obtain the maximum nourishment from what they eat, digesting it thoroughly. This chewing and re-chewing through the meditative process describes a turning over and over in the heart and mind the subject of our meditation, allowing the enzymes of the Holy Spirit to break down the truth and assimilate it into our lives.

> *Bruce Demarest writes concerning meditation, "Meditation is to cul-*
> *tivate the soil of the soul, which the traffic of the world compacts and*
> *hardens. The purpose of meditation is to permit the Holy Spirit to*
> *activate the living Word of God (and Divine truths of God) so that*
> *something more of our lives is transformed to bring us everyday, a little*
> *closer to the image of Christ."*[4]

Meditation involves selecting a word or phrase from the portion of scripture we are reading and choosing to sit with it before God, trusting that the Holy Spirit will teach us, will make the words and thoughts of God known to us as we ruminate. As you read or listen to scripture, pay attention to your internal feelings—is there a word or phrase you are drawn to, that seems to choose you? Or is there a word or phrase you feel resistance toward, that makes you feel challenged or uneasy? Both feelings are something to consider, each a type of burning bush that God is inviting you to turn aside and pay attention to. In your pondering and prayer, remain open to the ongoing leading and insights of the Spirit. I find it helpful to jot down what I hear and sense, and to try to carry it with me throughout my day.

If this is new to you, just spend five or ten minutes ruminating on a word or phrase that catches your attention, learning to trust God and to trust the process of opening your heart through meditation. As you experiment with the two types of meditation outlined below, see if you find one more helpful than another. Remember, the goal of meditation is to open your heart and mind to the ministry of the Spirit in order to encounter God.

MEDITATIVE PRACTICE ONE: LECTIO DIVINA

Lecto Divina means "sacred reading," but could more accurately be called "sacred listening." It has been practiced by Christians since the 6th century and was formalized in the 12th Century by the Carthusian monk Guigo II. A more complex form of meditation, it incorporates a variety of ways of interacting with God in scripture, and seeks to involve the whole person—heart, mind, body and spirit. Lectio Divina is reading for formation, not information; it is reading with the purpose of encountering the living God in such a way that one's heart and life are transformed.

Step 1: Select and slowly read a short passage of scripture, reading and re-reading until a word or phrase draws your attention through either attraction or resistance.

Step 2: Once you have identified a word or phrase, gently repeat that word or phrase to yourself. Receive and reflect on the thoughts, feelings, and images that come to you through this word or phrase. Allow these living words to interact with your attitudes, emotions and desires. How is God speaking? challenging? inviting? reminding or encouraging?

Step 3: Talk with God about what has surfaced as you ponder your word or phrase. Honestly express yourself, sharing openly your thoughts, feelings, and desires. Then listen for God's response.

Step 4: Rest completely in God, grateful for what has been given and for God's faithful presence surrounding you and indwelling you in abundant love.

Step 5: Ask God to help you embrace and live into and out of what's been made known to you during this time. This is a prayer of yielding and dependence, an admission of your need for grace and guidance.

In Lectio Divina, we give up control as we read the Scripture, and we become listeners, desiring to hear the still, small voice of God. The process may feel awkward at first, but once you learn the steps and settle into the experience, it promises a seamless conversation between you and God.

MEDITATIVE PRACTICE TWO: IMAGINATIVE PRAYER

When I refer to imaginative prayer I am speaking of the Spirit-infused, God-directed use of your imagination that enables the ability to experientially enter into the stories, symbolism, and images of the Bible. It empowers you to see and embrace the seen (physical) and the unseen (eternal). The Spirit-infused imagination moves you from sterile head-knowledge to life-transforming, heart-healing, biblically-informed living. As we embrace and employ our God-given, Spirit-infused imagination, we can more fully enter into the wonder and mystery of God's word. Imagination is not frivolous, evil, or childish; it is a gift from God.

The greatest validation of imagination as a tool for interacting with scripture is the Bible itself. In the opening chapters of Genesis the earth is formless and void, and the Spirit of God moves across its surface. Out of nothing but God's own imagination, light, sky, mountains, valleys, and all of life are created! The final book of Revelation is bursting with dramatic images and descriptions of Jesus, heaven, the turmoil of the world, and the birth of a new heaven and a new earth. From the first page of Scripture to the last, we fully engage imagination as a vehicle to transport us through this amazing story of creation and redemption, good versus evil, power, love, grace, and hope.

The Bible is written imaginatively because we are imaginative. These dramatic pictures exist to help us enter into the living word of God, to look beyond the seen to the unseen (2 Cor. 4:18), and to fully embrace the truth that in God we live, move, and have our being. Imagination gives us entrance into the mystery of God and God's word. We can imaginatively enter the Gospel stories using all of our senses; our imaginations allow us to be present, to see, smell, taste, touch, and hear what is unfolding. We don't just read about the manger, the garden, and the cross; we hear the cries of the newborn king, feel a Son's pain as he pleads with his Father, and see the nails driven into the tender flesh of our Savior.

In imaginative prayer, God speaks personally and powerfully in a deeply forming way, moving us from an external head-knowledge of God to an internal, experiential *knowing* of our personal Creator and Savior.

Step 1: Choose a story from the Bible. It's best to begin with an account from the Gospels when you are first learning this prayer practice, as they are more familiar and tend to be easy to understand, remember, and imagine.

Step 2: Read the story several times, paying attention to specifics. Notice the setting, the characters, and the situation. Who is the central figure? What is the problem? What is the outcome? What is unusual about this story? How does it connect with your life situation? Read the account enough times to understand its main point and to be familiar with the details.

Step 3: Imagine yourself as a participant in the story. You may be an onlooker or you may be involved in the action (as Mary, the leper, a disciple); put yourself* in that place and time. What do you see? smell? feel? hear? taste? think? Watch the situation as it unfolds. Be aware of your feelings, notice if you are drawn to something or resistant to doing something or going somewhere. Listen to what is said. What's your part in the conversation? Be open to making contact with Jesus, eye contact, a face-to-face encounter, a dialogue, just sitting with him. Pay attention to your feelings. Resist the temptation to interpret what's happening; simply be part of what's happening.

> *When you are in the story as one of the participants, it is you in the story. You are not trying figure out what they felt like, but are paying attention to your own feelings as Jesus heals you, an angel appears to you, Jesus says, "Follow me," etc.*

Step 4: Let your mind move slowly from the past to the present, taking with you the "feel" of the whole experience. Present your experience to God, openly and gratefully. Listen to God and remember all that happens is evaluated in light of the character and word of God. Put aside any images that are in opposition to God's character and word.

Not everyone has the same capacity for imagination. Some people are especially adept and can see a Biblical story clearly, even in vivid color. Don't be discouraged if you aren't one of them. The important thing is to make use of your imagination to the degree you are able and trust that God will honor your efforts. Be patient and gracious with yourself—have fun with it. Enter into the Gospel narratives with the freedom and playfulness of a child. God is with you.

FINAL THOUGHTS

Christian discernment involves recognizing the communications of God and learning to attend and respond to the Holy Spirit, which is exactly what these ways of interacting with God through scripture, outlined above, are designed to help foster within you.

EXERCISES:

1. Which of the ways to encounter God through scripture are you most drawn to, and which are you most resistant toward? Why?

2. During this week, choose to experiment with each of these ways of interacting with the scriptures. What did you hear or sense from God? What word, phrase, or knowing did you discover that you can carry with you through the rest of your day? Do not worry about doing these the "right" way, but instead embody a posture of playfulness, seeking to trust God and the process and see what happens.

SECTION FOUR: CHRISTIAN DISCERNMENT AND DECISION-MAKING

WARNING: If you read the Table of Contents and skipped to this section to discover more about discernment and decision-making, you're going to be disappointed. This isn't the solution you are looking for. Christian discernment and decision-making flow out of a practiced way of living Jesus that is a byproduct of embracing and internalizing the truths found in Section Two.

This section begins by presenting a couple of general Christian discernment and decision-making tips, before exploring a number of ways to partner with God in Christian discernment. It also points out the potential pitfalls involved in making decisions where intellect is the main player, and introduces the use of your imagination in Christian discernment and decision-making. When you aren't sensing God's leading, using your God-given imagination can open you to the promptings of the Spirit and God's wisdom. I have found two particular ways of using the imagination to be of great help when nothing else seems clear.

Throughout this section, we will be drawing from the insights of St Ignatius, a trusted expert when it comes to talking or writing about methods of discernment and decision-making. The section also includes an important chapter on the discernment of spirits. This discussion is meant to help you discern and understand the internal movements of the Spirit, in order to differentiate between the promptings of the Holy Spirit and those of Satan, the flesh, and/or the world—a critical knowing when it comes to Christian discernment.

CHAPTER TEN

CHRISTIAN DISCERNMENT INSIGHTS

C hances are you have been eager to reach this part of the book. There is something within us that wants a clear-cut series of steps regarding how something is to be done as well as some means for determining if we have in fact done it correctly. Discernment and decision-making are no different. However, from the beginning we have spoken about a different pathway of discernment. We even went so far as to abandon the term discernment, replacing it with "Christian discernment," emphasis on *Christian*. Christian discernment is an outflow of the work of the Spirit, an intentional way of life that fosters a deepening relationship with God, communion with Jesus, and attentiveness to the Spirit. It frees our hearts from disordered attachments (holy indifference) in order to respond to the leading and promptings of the Spirit.

But before (at last!) beginning our exploration of Christian discernment and decision-making, I want to look at three related insights. The first, if embraced, will help you avoid the trap of making hasty decisions without God's input. The second tip can help lower the level of stress and anxiety that often accompanies many of the so-called "big decisions" of life and enable you to open your ears to the Spirit and the eyes of your heart to God. The final insight reminds us that Christian discernment is an ongoing way of life.

Insight number one: When you are in a time of desolation, never change a decision you made in volitional consolation. Earlier in the book, we defined the terms desolation and consolation in two ways. The first had to do with affect, or our feelings. Consolations are interior movements in the soul, generated by an inflamed love for God, leading to increased hope, faith, love or joy. Desolation is all that is contrary to consolations—desolations are darkness of the soul, internal uneasiness, agitations, temptations, hopelessness and so on. The second definition concerned *volitional* consolation/desolation, i.e., not what we are feeling, but rather *where* a circumstance, internal feeling or interaction is taking us: toward God or away from God. Thus volitional consolation is defined as an interior and intentional movement toward God, and volitional desolation infers interior and intentional movement away from God—regardless of your feelings of pain or peace, comfort or confusion, joy or sadness.

Given these definitions, it would be quite foolish to change a decision you made when your life was flowing toward God and connected with God (volitional consolation) in a time when you are feeling distant from God, down, alone, unhappy, agitated, hopeless. Yet this is precisely when many people make changes in their lives. When they are unhappy with their current situation or life is not unfolding as they thought or hoped it would, they feel anxious, distraught, and alone. They decide it is time for a change. This is actually the worst time for them to make a new decision, as they are simply not internally able to discern God's will and fully avail themselves of the indispensable resources of God.

This simple and straightforward insight is extremely helpful. If you find yourself in desolation and desiring to make a change, invite God into your circumstances. Be open to how God may be working in your very situation to foster a deeper freedom within you, to be and become the person God has created and called you to be. Don't change the decision you made during a time of volitional consolation while you are struggling; instead cry out to God, seeking to put yourself in a place of connection with God where you are more likely to sense the often subtle promptings of the Holy Spirit. Then re-enter the discernment process using the modes of discernment we will cover in the next chapters.

Insight number two: Most of the decisions we make are changeable. People have a tendency to treat almost every decision as unchangeable, thereby creating for themselves HUGE, unnecessary pressure around decision-making. When I say decisions are changeable, I am not saying that change will be easy. In fact it may be costly, embarrassing, and even painful to change a changeable decision, but the truth is it can be done. The point is to stop treating every decision as if it is unchangeable. The vast majority of the decisions we make are of little more importance than "paper or plastic?"

The nature of an unchangeable decision, obviously, is that it *cannot* be changed. After such a decision is made, the only choice is to ask God to help you live out this decision in a God-honoring way, even if you realize that you made an unchangeable decision as a result of disordered attachments or wrong motives. This may seem a bit harsh, which is why it is extremely important to make unchangeable decisions using all the spiritual resources God makes available.

Thankfully, God will faithfully bring good out of an unchangeable decision whether you made it well-intentioned or poorly, because no decision can undermine the power, love, or grace of God. Because of the gravity of making unchangeable decisions, St. Ignatius, the expert on all things discernment, did not allow people to use the weighing of pros and cons in these most significant situations, believing this method did not provide the best opportunity to hear from God, to sense and lean on the promptings of the Spirit.

CHANGEABLE DECISIONS

The changeable decisions you make, although not as weighty as unchangeable decisions, need to be approached with a sober mind and a heart open to the communications of God in expected and unexpected places, as well as to the inner promptings of the Spirit. And though changeable decisions can be changed, the advice is to not change your decision too quickly. *If you have made a changeable decision in a God-honoring way, there is no reason to make a new decision*...UNLESS God directs you to change the changeable decision. This bring us to the next insight.

Insight number three: Christian Discernment is ongoing. Often when we think of changeable decisions, our focus is on our ability to change the decisions we make but the truth is that it is God who calls us to change decisions and not our own restlessness. The fact that most decisions are changeable is a reminder of the dynamic, free-flowing nature of life and also a reminder that yesterday's most excellent decision may not be the correct one for today. Christian discernment is an ongoing reality of life, a dynamic that brings to light a separation between Christian discernment and decision-making. *In decision-making there is a sense of finality to the process*—I made the decision and now it is time to move forward. Christian discernment, on the other hand, is ongoing, compelling us to be aware of the communications of God and the inner promptings of the Spirit. While we move forward embodying God's will, we continue to listen, to be aware, and to discern, knowing our changeable decisions are not set in stone; they're merely a step along the journey of living Jesus.

Sadly, many people make a changeable decision but never revisit it to discern if this is still the way God is leading. For example, a person begins a new job or starts attending graduate school—both changeable decisions. Unless something goes wrong, it is likely they will never discern if this remains the place God wants them to be. A changeable decision implies that God can move us from our job, our school, our neighborhood, even our church, and so we continue to seek God's ongoing leading to stay or go. The fact that a decision is changeable is a reminder that in time *God may initiate a change,* inviting/calling us to make a new decision, to embark on a new adventure.

Often what causes a person to revisit a changeable decision is the resulting hardship, adversity, or even misfortune that seems to be a by-product of that decision. This takes us back to our first insight: never change a decision made in a time of consolation when you are in desolation. What is called for in such cases is openness to God in your current experience, seeking to learn to trust God and trust the process. And once you are in a place of volitional consolation, open yourself to the possibility of changing and *then* re-enter the discernment process. And remember, immediate results, good or bad (from your perspective), do not determine whether your decision was correct or incorrect (bonus insight!). This often-used criterion for confirming a decision is faulty at best. Thus it is important to prayerfully process all of your circumstances with God, asking for God's wisdom and being indifferent to all but the embodiment of God's will—be it a meadow or a bullseye.

If you realize you made a changeable decision for all the wrong reasons, it does not necessarily mean that you will change your previous decision, only that you will re-enter the discernment process. You may very well have made the correct decision for the wrong reasons. So you re-discern your changeable decision, learning from your past mistakes and open to how God is using your current situation to mold and shape you and further teach you about discernment. Only in that openness will you know if God may be leading you toward change.

Later, in Section Five, we will present several more discernment insights, but for now, let these last reminders suffice:

- never change a decision made in a time of volitional consolation during a time of desolation.
- there are two types of decisions: changeable and unchangeable.
- since most decisions are changeable, you need to always be discerning, open to God's leading.
- the perceived outcomes of decisions are not trustworthy guides regarding whether or not you made a God-honoring decision.

EXERCISES:

1. Look over your life and see if there are any changeable decisions that you are treating as unchangeable, not asking or maybe even not open to asking God if it is time to make a change. If there are, what is behind your unwillingness to be open and willing to change? Share you feelings with God.

2. Are you in a period of affective desolation and desperately desiring to make a change, yet not sensing God's guidance? Ask God to help you open your heart in this difficult time, to teach you to learn to trust God's love, goodness, grace, and mercy even if you may not be feeling it. Express your feelings and frustrations with God, knowing God hears you and that nothing separates you from God's love.

3. As you reviewed your current changeable decisions—job, living situation, school, areas you are serving in, groups you belong to—are you sensing God's invitation in a new direction? Is there an invitation to begin to discern with God regarding some possible changes? If so, what are you sensing from God? How do you know it is from God?

CHAPTER ELEVEN

CHRISTIAN DISCERNMENT: WHAT DOES IT LOOK LIKE?

L et's start with what it's not: Christian discernment is not a clearly defined process. Now, here's what it is: Christian discernment is an openness of heart to the Spirit and to the communications of God in expected and unexpected places. Built on the knowledge that God is personally involved in the lives of God's children, it flows from a practiced way of life that fosters a deep and growing relationship with God. Christian discernment is hugely relational, and thus personal in nature.

Before we get too far, I think it's important to address an often unasked question: Who initiates the discernment process? Is the initiator a human person (you or me), or is it the Holy Spirit? The answer, at least in practice, seems to be that a human person is the initiator. The individual has a decision that needs to be made and brings it before God, asking for God to lead him or her through the discernment/decision-making process, and then offers the decision to God, desiring an external indication or sign that God agrees with the resulting decision. Yet, this is neither the way of Christian discernment nor the way one finds God leading people in the Bible.

As we look at the decision-makers in scripture, we do not find people agonizing over their dilemmas, begging God for clarity about a decision they have made or need to make, incorporating common sense while weighing pros and cons, or, as a rule, asking for signs of confirmation—except in the case of Gideon, who actually doubted the confirming sign he received and asked for another (not exactly the confirmation he desired). No, throughout Scripture we find God taking the initiative. Then the ones who encounter God must choose to respond or not to respond to God's proactive leading.

Noah was not pondering the building of a large boat; Abram was not weighing the pros and cons of moving; Moses not brainstorming about leading Israel to the promised land; nor was Gideon considering a move from farmer to judge, or David plotting a career path that would lead him to the throne. And later in history, Mary was planning her wedding, not mulling over giving birth to the son of God; James and John were fishing, not planning to become apostles; Paul was riding on a donkey, not contemplating giving up persecuting Christians to become one. In each of these cases, the person was living a normal life when God broke in. The key to discernment for each was not a streamlined formulaic methodology, rather the ability to recognize the communications of God (in whatever form they arrived) and to have a heart predisposed to follow where they sensed God's leading—even if it was a struggle. I'm reminded of the words of Jesus, when he pointed out that he did whatever he saw the Father doing (John 5:19). Jesus joined in, once he knew what the Father was up to.

So if God is the initiator and we are to respond, what does this look like as we live our daily lives? The first order of business is the cultivation of ongoing awareness, especially regarding the communications of God and promptings of the Spirit, and, secondly, a heart freed from disordered loves and predisposed to embodying God's will (see Section Two). With these predispositions in mind, let's turn our attention to two modes of Christian discernment developed by Ignatius. Both flow from a belief that God is involved in our lives and does not play games when it comes to disclosing his will, whether it be a meadow or bullseye—*especially* when it's a bullseye. God is proactive in making God's will known to us through the Spirit that indwells us. God is the initiator and we are called to be ready to respond.

TWO MODES OF CHRISTIAN DISCERNMENT

Mode One: The "Pyrotechnic Mode"

Mode One is dramatic, the experience of all the bells and whistles that many so desire when making choices. As I have walked alongside people in their decision-making process, I've seen that many long for some undeniable sign from God that will assure them that they have made the correct choice, calming all their worries and fears. Yet scripture doesn't show us individuals asking for signs or asking if a certain sign is God's doing. Any such confirmation usually comes after the fact. The truth is—and this is another discernment insight to add to your list—*every decision we make will always involve faith, risk, and the unknown. What we do know for certain is that God is with us, committed to us, and forever faithful to us.*

Ignatius gives two examples of what I call the pyrotechnic mode. The first example is Paul's encounter with Jesus, which led him to turn from a Jesus-persecutor to a Jesus-follower. Paul was not looking for change at this point, but God broke in unannounced and uninvited. The event is recorded is Acts 9, and here are some of the pyrotechnic details: a light shines from heaven, Paul is knocked to the ground, a voice sounds from heaven, Paul asks a question, Jesus responds, and in the process Paul is struck blind. This is wild stuff! Any of us, including Paul, would have no doubt that something significant just happened and we need to be ready to respond. This is what many desire when it comes to discernment—except the being blinded part—but as we read more about Paul's life, we do not see this type of leading ever again. Yet Paul is continually led by the Spirit, continually seeking to partner with what the Father was doing. As exciting and attractive as pyrotechnics may be to some, they are not the norm when it comes to God's leading.

A second example of this mode of Christian discernment is found in Matthew 9, the calling of Mathew the tax collector. Although Ignatius links these two encounters, they are very different, at least on the surface. In the Matthew passage there is no bright light, no voice from heaven, no exchange, no blindness; there is a simple interaction—invitation and response. Jesus says to Matthew, "Follow me," and Matthew obediently follows. I believe Ignatius found a common denominator between the encounters of Paul and Matthew in the fact that both were a powerful internal experience, a knowing of God that could not be explained away, but had to be responded to if one was to be true to the experience. The pyrotechnics of this mode are an internal reality, whether or not there are also external spiritual fireworks.

This mode is beautifully portrayed in Elijah's encounter with God recorded in 1 Kings 19:11–13. Elijah waited for God but did not experience God in a powerful, mighty way. God appeared to Elijah not in the strong wind, the earthquake, or the fire, but rather as a gentle whisper. Elijah could have missed God, as I think many of us do while waiting for the spectacular. We miss the simple, profound whisper of God—a whisper, which if truly heard in our hearts, can shake our very foundations. Hearing God's pyrotechnic, foundation-altering whisper takes hearing ears and an open, responsive heart, an expectant awareness of the here-and-now as we wait for God.

Mode Two: The "Inner Promptings"

The second mode involves the receiving of enough spiritual light and insight through one's internal awareness of consolations and desolations, as well as a sensitivity to the movement of spirits (evil, flesh, the world), and the Holy Spirit in order to arrive at a deeper inner knowing of God's leading—God's will.

Apparently the predominant way God invites us to make decisions, Mode Two is a direct byproduct of Jesus' gift of the Spirit; it's an internal awareness of the stirrings of our heart and the presence of the Spirit. Awareness of the volitional consolations (taking us to God) and volitional desolations (taking us away for God), along with affect consolations (inflamed by the love of God, increasing in hope, faith, love, and interior joy, seeking the things above) and affect desolation (turmoil of spirit, movement to low and earthly things, lack of faith or hope or love, laziness, sadness and distance from God), provide us with insight into how God is leading us from the good to the best.

Mode Two is entered into when you become aware of a choice to be made—an opportunity for a new job, desire to buy a house, invitation to serve in the community or at church, the possibility of a new venture—and you do not experience Mode One. In Mode Two, you immediately pay attention to the inner promptings of the Spirit and to what you are sensing inside: resistance, dread, joy, excitement, gratitude, confusion. Owning who you are in Christ and mindful of the predispositions that take you away from God, you use the inner promptings of the Spirit to turn your attention to God.

When you can know and name your disordered attachments/loves that exercise some level of control over you, you are able to make allowances for them. I love comfort, and I equate it with well-being and security, so when I receive an invitation or opportunity that I immediately sense will involve additional demands, sacrifice, and hard work, it generates desolation in me, and my initial response is a strong internal resistance both to saying yes and to hearing God out. But because I know that I am able to invite God into my discomfort, my affect desolation begins to turn into volitional consolation, enabling me to be open to God's wisdom, perceive the inner movements of the Spirit, and move toward a posture of holy indifference. Christian discernment is not about being perfect but aware—God-aware and self-aware.

INNER MOVEMENT OF THE SPIRIT

What do the inner movements of the Spirit feel like? St Ignatius offers two pictures to depict the subtle movements of the Spirit and these help us to know when we are moving from good to best. The images, which we've examined before, are a drop of water hitting a sponge, and a drop of water hitting a rock. If within your spirit what you *hear/sense* feels like a drop of water gently landing on a sponge, you know that this is of God. Conversely, if what you *hear/sense* feels jarring, repelled rather than absorbed—like a drop of water hitting a stone—it is not of God. The difference can be very subtle.

To illustrate this subtlety, I would again invite you to fold your hands by interlacing your fingers. Now switch the position of your thumbs, paying attention to how each position feels. One way seems right to you and the other not. It is not a glaring difference, but still noticeable. Such is the subtlety of the drop of water hitting a sponge or a stone. When you begin to recognize and trust your inner promptings, you will be able to more quickly sense the Spirit's lead in the to-and-fro of life.

When it comes to discerning the inner movements of the Spirit, two helpful words to keep in mind are *drawn* and *driven*. When the Spirit of God is leading us, there is a sense of being drawn into something. "Drawn" does not mean the resulting decision will be easy or even something you want to do, but deep down there is a peace, an ease, a knowing that this invitation is from God. Conversely, when you are feeling driven, forced, even coerced, it is not of God. It is important to remember that if these inner stirrings are truly Spirit-led, they will never be in conflict with the revealed truths of scripture or the person and character of God.

This internal awareness is not always immediate. There are times you will need to carry the decision within you, paying attention to the feelings that are stirring, awaiting clarity from the Spirit. This is especially true if you live a fast-paced, hectic life. It will take time to allow things to settle. The tendency will be to immediately jump to the use of pros and cons, but I urge you to not embrace that mode of decision-making too quickly. As you will discover in chapter 13, a list of pros and cons is not all that reliable when it comes to discerning and embodying God's will. Instead, take some time to sit with your choice, gently turning it over in your heart, even using one or more of the imaginative exercises found in Chapter 14 to help you open to God and to the inner promptings of the Spirit.

This holding a decision and gently turning it over in my heart, seeking to be sensitive to the Spirit, has played out in my own life many times. Once I was asked to write a journal article. I do not see myself as a writer and knew that it would take a lot of work to cover the material adequately in the allotted space, so my initial internal response was, "NO! I do not want to do this." But knowing my strong desire for comfort and my tendencies to avoid what seems difficult, I did not immediately say no. Instead I asked for time (time is a great friend when it comes to discerning and decision-making) to ponder the opportunity and carry the choices within me. As I opened to God and began to listen for the inner promptings of the Spirit, that drop of water gently landed on a sponge. It became quite clear that I was to write the article.

The focus of Mode Two is the internal awareness of the communications of God, the stirrings of the spirits, and, most importantly, the promptings of the Spirit. It doesn't mean the catalyst of this inner awareness cannot come from the outside—the reading of scripture, the words of another, a song, a book, even a movie. The emphasis in this mode is one's internal response to promptings, wherever they originate. At various times in my life, God has spoken through people regarding a decision I was carrying in my heart. Although they had no idea of their impact, I knew in the moment that God was communicating to me as I sensed the promptings of the Spirit.

Dallas Willard speaks to this mode of Christian discernment: "The final instrumentality…through which God addresses us is our own spirits—our own thoughts and feelings, toward ourselves as well as toward events and people around us. And this, I believe, is the primary subjective mode through which God addresses us."[1]

DISCERNMENT AS A WAY OF LIFE

Christian discernment is dependent on God; it is energized and empowered by the Spirit and its use is not limited to the big decisions of life. Yet too often discernment is relegated to those BIG decisions, without any thought given to the hundreds of little ones made everyday that mold and shape who we are. One reason is that our go-to decision-making process involves a listing and weighing of pros and cons, and this is a ponderous practice that would be impossible to implement with the myriad of daily choices. But as we learn to walk by the Spirit, sensitive to the inner moments of the Spirit, aware of the subtlety of a drop of water landing on a sponge or hitting a rock, we can begin to live with a SPIRIT-INFUSED-SPONTANEOUS-INCISIVENESS, able to be in the moment, open to and following God's leading consciously and subconsciously in our daily life. This is the life Jesus speaks of in John 3, when he describes those born of the Spirit as the wind; you do not know where they are coming from or where they are going, but you feel their power. Bob Mumford says, "When Christ's abiding presence becomes our guide, then guidance becomes an almost unconscious response to the gentle moving of the Holy Spirit within us."[2] As a result we are able to live freely and lightly, embracing the unforced rhythms of God's Spirit.

Once aware that the key is to trust these promptings of the Spirit, you are free to act in the moment, trusting that God is involved in leading and guiding you as you remain open. A name pops into your mind and you're prompted to pray, text, email, write a note; as you enter a room, you sense a need to sit in a particular place, talk to a certain person; you immediately know you need to say no or yes to a specific invitation or opportunity. The struggle comes in trusting those inner promptings enough to act.

Once when I was leading a retreat, on two separate occasions I knew I was to say something specific to one person and to pat another on the shoulder. Both promptings were quite subtle, but I knew God was leading me, so I did what I sensed God telling me to do. It was the first time anything like that had ever happened to me, and I am grateful that at least once I chose to act on God's prompt. As a result, over the years I am more open and more responsive to those subtle movements of the Spirit within.

These two modes of Christian discernment involve a total dependency and yielded-ness to God and the Spirit of God, who is actively leading us, guiding us, making God's words, thoughts, and wisdom known to us. As we become more keenly aware of how God communicates with us, with the sound of God's voice, and the subtlety of the Spirit's prompting, as well becoming more aware of our own tendency toward certain temptations and delusions, we will more and more be able to embody God's will in all the decisions of life. We will be like those born of the Spirit, wind-blown here and there by the power of the Spirit, living in the moment a life characterized by a *Spirit-infused-spontaneous-incisiveness.*

CONFIRMATION

In Modes One and Two, there is no mention of seeking or needing confirmation, for confirmation is implied in the interaction with God and not independent of it. This lack of an additional external confirmation is a roadblock for many, who stall while waiting for a sign they are on the right path before proceeding. They long for a Red Sea type of experience, where the waters part first and *then* they proceed (Ex. 14:15ff), but as we mature in our faith, we are invited into a Jordan crossing experience (Josh. 3:1ff), where there is no parting of the river *until* one is standing in it. This Spirit-led action necessitates a level of Christian maturity not always seen by Paul and the writers of Hebrews in the followers of Jesus (1 Cor. 3:1–3, Heb. 5:11–14), a maturity resulting from a practiced way of life that fosters the ability to more fully and completely trust God.

EXERCISES:

1. Which of the two modes of Christian discernment are you most comfortable with? Why? Which have you experience in your own life? Describe the occurrence.

2. Have there been times in your life when you, at least initially, thought you sensed an inner prompting of the Spirit described above in Mode Two? If yes, what did it feel like? What made you think it was from God? Did you choose to follow the leading? Why or why not?

3. If you have not had that inner sense of the Spirit's leading, are you open to experiencing it? If yes, ask God to help you open your heart and deepen your sensitivity to the subtle movement of the Spirit. Also, you may want to go back over the chapter entitled "Be Aware."

CHAPTER TWELVE

DISCERNMENT OF SPIRITS

When seeking to live life in Modes One and Two of Christian discernment, it is important to learn the often-subtle yet distinct characteristics that confirm the movements of the Holy Spirit amidst the other spirits that seek to keep you from embodying God's will. The insights presented in this chapter will help you learn to become aware of and recognize contrary spirits, their strategies, and their schemes in order to lessen their influence in the discernment process. These insights also serve as a sober reminder of the spiritual reality in which we live. Peter talks about our need to "be sober-minded; be watchful [for] your adversary the devil prowls around like a roaring lion, seeking someone to devour" (1 Peter 5:8). Paul writes: "…we do not wrestle against flesh and blood, but against the rulers, against the authorities, against the cosmic powers over this present darkness, against the spiritual forces of evil in the heavenly places" (Eph. 6:12).

This chapter will help you to be wise as serpents as you test and identify the stirring of the spirit within, whether it is God's Spirit or those spirits contrary to God, and to act accordingly—resisting or embracing. This need to test the spirits is echoed in Scripture as well. "Beloved, do not believe every spirit, but test the spirits to see whether they are from God..." (1 John 4:1a) and Paul writes, "Do not quench the Spirit...but test everything; hold fast what is good" (I Thess. 5:19, 21).

INSIGHTS FOR DISCERNMENT OF SPIRITS

The following insights have been adapted from Ignatius' rules for discernment of spirits and have serious implications when it comes to Christian discernment and the use of Mode Two.

1. Satan can and does appear as an angel of light (2 Cor. 11:14) and will even use good and holy thoughts to bring about evil. As we have matured in Christ, knowing good from evil, Satan is forced to change his strategy. He moves from tempting us with overt evil and starts seeking to twist the good using *false reasons, subtleties, and persistent fallacies* and will even acquiesce to entrapping us in the good to keep us from the best. The means Satan uses will not be obvious and unreasonable—they will make sense on some level and may even appear to be wise—and he will have a dogged determination to keep you from embodying God's will.

   An example of this is affect consolation. When affect consolation has an external cause (music, Scripture, a sunset, a child's smile, a work of art, a sermon, a Bible passage), it can come from God or from an evil spirit. It can no longer be assumed that affect consolation is a gift from God even when it arises from a good and godly source.

   Note: If you experience affect consolation *without an external cause*, it can be fully trusted because only God can create ex nihilo (out of nothing); Satan can only twist that which already exists. This type of affect consolation comes with a surprising suddenness—in a moment one is overwhelmed by the love, grace, joy, and/or peace of God. It may last for a single moment or linger for a while. Either way it is a profound experience to be savored and enjoyed—soak in it, drink it in with abandonment. It is pure gift.

2. The evil one may begin by suggesting thoughts that are suited to a devout soul, but *little by little* he achieves his ends and perverse intentions.

The phrase "little by little" is used to highlight that this seduction could take weeks, months, even years to happen. Let me give you an illustration from my own life. Years ago I began to go barefoot as a result of reading Exodus 3. My intention was that it would remind me that everywhere I step, God is there, and to also represent a grounding in God. I went barefoot for years. One day I was waiting for someone to arrive and a student engaged me in a conversation that God used to expose how I had veered from my original course. Along the way, not wearing shoes had become a mark of my identity, a badge of honor. I was shocked to acknowledge how my original intention had been waylaid. It happened little by little over a significant time, and I was quite unaware anything had changed until the chance conversation occurred. Once again, this is a reminder of the need for ongoing discernment.

The suggested thoughts and affect consolations crafted by Satan are a Trojan horse designed for your undoing. Dean Brackley points out that they "are tailor-made to your weaknesses, targeting your moral strengths [seeking to exaggerate them]and your psychological weaknesses [compulsions, disordered loves]."[1] This truth highlights your need for self-awareness. As you become aware of your predisposition toward certain disordered attachments, you can then choose to move more slowly, more earnestly seeking the leading of the Spirit and asking for God's wisdom.

Now, a piece of good news: you can escape the devil's trap before it is fully sprung by employing the last four insights on this list.

3. While making a decision, and after making it, be aware of and continue to pay attention to the progression of your heart and thoughts—are they still in harmony with scripture, the fruits of the Spirit, the person of Jesus? If the beginning, middle, and end is all good or inclined toward good—manifesting the fruit of the Spirit (Gal. 5:22–23)—it is a sign of God's leading. But if, as you are decision-making and decision-enacting, your heart and thoughts drift

toward distraction, or if your thoughts weaken, disquiet, or trouble the soul, or if the deeds of the flesh (Gal. 5:19–21) are beginning to manifest within you then you have some clear signs that these proceed from an evil spirit. Something that starts out good, like not wearing shoes, can little by little be distorted, but the erosion can be detected and redirected if you are paying attention and are open to the ongoing leading of the Spirit in expected (e.g., God's word) and unexpected (e.g., a random conversation) ways. God will never abandon you, but will always seek to set you back on course—thus it is important to have ears to hear what the Spirit is saying.

4. When you realize you have been deceived, retrace the course of your thoughts. Go back to the beginning, middle, and end of your choice, exploring your attitudes to see where the evil spirit got its claws in you.

Once God made me aware of how my original reason for going barefoot had been subverted, I was able to look back, with God's help, and see that I had actually become a slave to not wearing shoes. The awareness of how it felt when my not wearing shoes started going sideways has helped me in other situations to sense when a shift is beginning to take place, enabling me to explore my heart, reconnect with God, and seek God's wisdom and insight moving forward. Taking the time to retrace your steps, the progression of your heart, and your thoughts will help you become more quickly aware of the subtle changes within you in the future.

The truth is that Satan cannot perfectly camouflage what he is doing. In the words of Ignatius you will "see the serpent's tail" and be able to take appropriate action as God leads and empowers you.

So when you "see the serpent's tail" and realize you're off-track, it's important to take it to God, acknowledging your need for wisdom and insight before moving forward. Resist the temptation to merely react by trying to make it right on your own. When I realized that my not wearing shoes had been turned from something God-honoring to something self-prompting, my first reaction was to buy some shoes. I went online to order a pair, but as I was doing so, I realized I had not yet brought this matter to God. As I began to pray, I was immediately aware of the serpent's tail in my over-reaction. I needed to take time—once again please note *the importance of time in discernment*—and talk with God before jumping into action. I ended up not buying shoes, but I am no longer enslaved to going barefoot. Now I occasionally wear shoes and often wear socks. I regained freedom in this area and can now enjoy being barefoot for the right, God-honoring reasons—and I am also paying attention to the course of my thoughts and heart as I continue to walk barefooted with Jesus. When you become aware that you are off course, don't try to self-correct. Turn to God, asking for wisdom and direction, and then keep discerning.

5. This is my favorite insight and it has been mentioned in previous chapters. When you are proceeding from good to better, you will experience God's touch as light and gentle, like a drop of water gently falling on a sponge, a deep sense this is right and good—to me it is like what I feel when I put on a soft pair of socks or my flannel pajama bottoms, it is a deep sense of inner goodness—this is the way it is supposed to be. Please don't misunderstand me: I do not mean it will be an easy path to follow. Rather, I am speaking of a deep knowing within that this is right and good and God is leading you to move forward no matter where you are being led—to a place of honor or through the valley of the shadow of death.

Conversely, when you are going in the other direction—good to bad or less good—you will experience the evil spirits like a drop of water hitting a stone: sharp, dissonant, producing inner disquiet. This is a deep sense that something is just not quite right, like when you are trying on a new pair of shoes and though they are the correct size, they do not feel right on your feet, and you put them back. It is this subtle knowing that *this opportunity is not quite right.* You may or may not be able to name why you feel the way you do, but you know deep within that this is not something God is inviting you into. As you become more proficient in discerning the subtle difference between these drops of water, you will be less likely to fall into the snares of the devil.

6. This final insight takes you all the way back to the note above on *consolation without an external cause*. Be careful to distinguish the euphoria of the consolation without previous cause from the afterglow you will feel after the consolation without previous cause is over. During the afterglow, the enemy will seek to rush in, to convince you to make heartfelt commitments and vows to God that appear to be God-honoring. Do not make any decision or vows immediately after an experience of consolation without previous cause. Just enjoy it as the gift of pure grace, for that is what it is.

FINAL THOUGHTS

You can see that the strategies of the evil one are subtle and sophisticated. It is extremely important for you to be vigilant, evaluating and reevaluating consolations, evaluating and reevaluating good and holy thoughts, paying attention to the beginning, middle, and ends of the decisions you make to discern their origin and determine if they continue to bring honor and glory to God. Are they the manifestation of the fruits of the Spirit or are they now satisfying the needs of the flesh, leading to self-aggrandizement and taking you away from God and the purposes of God?

As you become more familiar with these insights, sensitive to the prompting of the Spirit, and able to distinguish between the Spirit (a drop of water gently landing on a sponge) and the other spirits (drops of water hitting a rock), you will more readily be able to make use of Mode Two in Christian discernment and to live in the freedom of Spirit-infused-spontaneous-incisiveness. If you are feeling a bit overwhelmed by these insights and even a little fearful, share your feelings with God, knowing God is with you. And remember that as crafty as Satan may be, he is not able to perfectly camouflage himself. He can be spotted by the "serpent's tail" and the corresponding deeds of the flesh that will arise within you when you begin to stray—keep your eyes and ears open and God will lead and guide you.

EXERCISES:

1. Which of the insights found in this chapter seem to be most helpful to you? Why?

2. Which of the insights is the most difficult for you to get your head around? Why?

3. How are you doing as far as developing your internal awareness of the drop of water gently landing on a sponge or hitting a rock? What practices might you incorporate into your life to help develop a greater sensitivity to the drop of water (see chapter 5)?

CHAPTER THIRTEEN

DECISION-MAKING: PROS AND CONS

In Chapter 11 we looked closely at the two modes of Christian discernment, and in both of these modes God is the lead player in the action. There is a third mode of discernment, but, while widely used by both Christians and non-Christians, it is vastly different in that the intellect replaces the Spirit as the primary player. In fact, it is the very absence of an overt leading by God that brings one to a place of even considering the use of Mode Three to make a decision.

An apt analogy of the difference between the first two modes and Mode Three is found in Matthew 16 in an exchange between Jesus and Peter about the identity of Jesus and his impending death. Jesus asks Peter, "Who do you say that I am?" and Peter responds, "You are the Christ, the Son of the living God" (Matt. 16:15–16). Jesus then declares that this truth was not revealed to Peter by "flesh and blood...but [by] my Father who is in heaven" (Matt. 16:17). A perfect example of Modes One and Two: God in the lead. If you recall, Mode One has God acting independently of us, breaking into our daily life and inviting us to follow; in Mode Two we are partnering with God, attending to the communications of God, becoming aware of the promptings of the Spirit in order to discern God's leading. Modes One and Two are fully and firmly anchored in God.

Mode Three is seen in the next exchange between Jesus and Peter, when Jesus speaks of his impending death and Peter responds, "Far be it from you, Lord! This shall never happen to you" (Matt. 16:22). Jesus responds, "...you are not setting your mind on the things of God, but on the things of man" (Matt. 16:23b). And here lies the inherent danger. Because Mode Three relies so heavily on the use of one's intellect, it is easy to lose sight of the concerns of God and to be influenced instead by preoccupations with culture and society, assumptions about what is right and good, the knowledge of what needs to be done and what seems humanly wise, productive, efficient, and in harmony with the resources currently available. In Mode Three it is easy for the concerns of God to be eclipsed by human concerns, goals, and wisdom.

Thomas Green, in comparing what I have referred to as Mode 2 and 3 writes, "It is, to put it quite simply, the difference between guessing what my friend is thinking [Mode Three] and hearing him say what he is thinking [Modes One and Two]."[1]

Yet Mode Three remains the go-to mode of decision-making for most people. Drawn in by the desire to be in control of the process, people have not cultivated the knowledge of God and self, or the practice of holy indifference and awareness that enables them to be more fully in tune with the inner promptings of the Holy Spirit and the communications of God. They depend instead upon reason and their own intellect, neither of which is even mentioned in Modes One and Two, and they follow the path of least resistance, even when it is problematic. Doing what seems reasonable does not necessarily equate to being in God's will (see Chapter 20, "Heart and Head"). Paul reminds us that the *apparent foolishness of God* is wiser than man's wisdom (1 Cor. 1:25). Because of the emphasis on reason some view Mode Three as deficient, "Spirit-lite."

I am not saying that Mode Three is always an unacceptable method of decision-making, but rather pointing out that the use of pros and cons is fraught with difficulties and is not the go-to Mode of Christian discernment that many make it out to be. Ignatius saw it as the Mode of last resort, only to used when Modes One or Two are seemingly inaccessible. Ignatius offers the following caveats when using pros and cons:

- *Only use this Mode when you are unable to make a decision using Mode One or Mode Two.* This is a reminder that this is not your first choice when seeking to discern God's leading.

- *Never use Mode Three to make an unchangeable decision.* This caveat is a clear sign of Mode Three's untrustworthy nature. Even in the case of a changeable decision, it is the mode of last resort.

- *Remain indifferent, free from all disordered attachments, loves, and desires that exert undo pressure on your ability to freely say yes to God.* Ignatius states this twice. When employing Mode Three, it is difficult to keep the concerns of God above personal concerns and desires.

- *Remember to choose that which brings God greater glory and honor.* Well-aware of how easy it is to adopt an alternate goal when not being led by the Spirit, Ignatius warns of this human tendency four times.

The above reminders highlight the dangers and concerns associated with Mode Three, but Ignatius also provides four positive suggestions to help us when we find ourselves making a decision that calls for the of use pros and cons:

1. Ask God to move your will and open your heart to what you ought to choose: that which is for the praise and glory of God. This opening prayer is an important step, owning your limitations of intellect and the need for God's wisdom and guidance—even when you are not currently experiencing God's leading. Recall the passage in James, "If any of you lacks wisdom, let him ask God, who gives generously to all without reproach, and it will be given him. But let him ask in faith, with no doubting..." (1:5–6a). God is with you even though you may not be sensing the leading of the Spirit in the moment, so continue to invite God into the process with you, en-

deavoring to "Trust in the Lord with all your heart, and do not lean on your own understanding. In all your ways acknowledge him..." (Prov. 3:5–6). The prayer is that God will be present and ultimately influence the decision.

2. Keeping the issue before you, consider and weigh the advantages and disadvantages on each side. This is IMPORTANT—it is not one list of pros and cons, but two lists: What are the pros and cons of a yes, and what are the pros and cons of a no? And there's more... once you have listed the advantages and disadvantages of each side of the issue, you then weigh them, assigning a level of importance to each of the pros and cons. As you will discover, they are not all equal, an important factor as you make your decision. The decision is not reached as a result of one list being longer than the other, but rather as a result of the importance of the considerations on a particular list. For example, if your list of pros regarding a yes was extremely long, but you also know that if you say yes, it would not lead to the greater praise and glory of God—a HUGE con, then the answer needs to be a no. The weightiness of that one piece outweighs everything else on the other side. An honest evaluation of the various criteria on each list is extremely important, which is why it is important to be indifferent, keeping the ultimate goal of God's greater praise and glory in the forefront of your mind.

3. Once you have completed listing and weighing the pros and cons, it is time to make a decision. Remember, you are not deciding between good and evil, and this decision is one that is changeable. It may very well be more of a meadow-type decision than a bulls-eye decision, meaning God may allow you to choose either while remaining in the meadow of God's will.

4. Having made your decision, it is time to seek God's confirmation. This is not a formality but a necessity, because as stated earlier, this mode is fraught with danger. This crucial step can take a while, which is why time is an important component in Christian discernment. Ignatius once took a full week before sensing God's confirmation of a decision he made using pros and cons. The importance of God's confirmation in the process cannot be minimized. Actually,

the hope is that this opening to God may lead into a Mode One or Two experience, where God's presence is made known in an unmistakable way. But if that's not the case, we are left to face the important question, "What does confirmation look like?"

Some wrongly look externally for confirmation—circumstances are favorable for implementing the decision; the decision has an excellent chance of accomplishing what is desired; or the means and resources needed to make the decision are readily available. While each of these is a reasonable assessment, they are NOT proper confirmation. Others see confirmation as an experience of peace and well-being, but this feeling can just as easily be a result of the final decision being aligned with our human desires. Think of Jesus in the garden praying to the Father to avoid the cross, sweating drops of blood. Jesus was not experiencing peace or well-being but torment, yet he knew what he was to do and prayed, "not as I will but as you [God] will" (Matt. 26:36ff).

Confirmation, when it comes, will produce in some form an internal expression of the fruit of the Spirit—love, joy, peace, patience, kindness, goodness, faithfulness, gentleness, and self-control (Gal. 5:22–23), along with the characteristics of the wisdom from above, the wisdom of God—pure, peace-loving, considerate, submissive, full of mercy and good fruit, impartial and sincere (James 3:17). It doesn't mean there won't be some anxiety, concern or nervousness when moving into the decision, but beneath those often valid feelings, there is a peace, a gentleness, a submitting to God and trusting of God. It is the reality of being grounded in a deep knowing of the goodness and faithfulness of God that may be experienced like a drop of water gently landing on a sponge, the interior knowing that this is right. As with all changeable decisions, discernment doesn't end, but continues after the decision is made, because it is likely that sooner or later God will invite you into another time of discernment about the very thing you have just decided. Your ongoing holy indifference, awareness, and openness to the leading of God and the prompting of the Spirit continues, for Christian discernment is a way of life.

Above we spoke of the limitations inherent in Mode Three and to those

I would like to add another: Mode Three, while being an acceptable way to make decisions in certain situations, is not useful for the hundreds of decisions you make daily. And since for many, Mode Three is the only way decisions are consciously made, it can be hard to even fathom a practical way for a person to be led by the Spirit throughout the day. But it's actually not as impossible as it seems. We have the Spirit within us to guide and direct. As we continue to order our lives in a way that is open to the communications of God and the promptings of the Spirit, we are able to bring a Spirit-infused-spontaneous-incisiveness to living, and to the hundreds of decisions we make each day. Our daily decisions can promote God's greater glory and serve God's purpose as the natural flow of a godly life rightly ordered.

When it comes to Christian discernment, we have much more available to us than the listing and weighing of pros and cons. We have access to wisdom from above, the inner leading of the Spirit, the words and thoughts of God. Yet too often the go-to mode—weighing pros and cons—is allowed to thwart the development and deepening of our ability to become aware of and sensitive to the movements of God that are characteristic of Modes One and Two. We are cut off from the ability to embody God's unfolding will in the coming and goings of everyday life.

EXERCISES:

1. With which of the three Modes of Christian discernment and decision-making are you most comfortable? Why?

2. With which of the three Modes of Christian discernment and decision-making are you least comfortable? Why?

3. As you reflect on Jesus' life, which of the three Modes do you see that he relied on most and which did he rely on least?

4. Why do you think the pros and cons method of decision-making is so popular among Christians?

CHAPTER FOURTEEN

IMAGINATION AND CHRISTIAN DISCERNMENT

The use of your God-given imagination is helpful when used in conjunction with Mode Three, especially at those times when you are not sensing God's leading, not fully confident in your use of pros and cons, or when seeking the needed confirmation before finalizing a decision made in Mode Three. When using your imagination, Ignatius reminds you (as he also did in Mode Three) to embrace holy indifference so that, motivated solely by the love of God, you are able to choose that which will lead to God's greater glory.

I have personally experienced the benefits of using imagination in circumstances where I did not sense God's leading, and the weighing and sifting through pros and cons proved less than helpful. The use of imagination can create in us the distance necessary to see a situation more clearly. It can also put us in touch with our core beliefs and values, which we often fail to even consider in the decision-making process of weighing pros and cons. Additionally, employing our God-given imagination may ultimately open our hearts to the inner movements of the Spirit, an indirect path into the certainty of Mode Two.

IMAGINE...SUGGESTIONS FROM IGNATIUS

1. Imagine someone in your exact circumstances comes to you for advice about the same decision with which you are wrestling. What would you tell that person to do next? I found this imaginative exercise extremely helpful when I was discerning whether or not to leave my pastoral position to launch b, my spiritual formation ministry. When I engaged my imagination in the question, I immediately knew what to do next. In my case, it wasn't that I immediately arrived at an answer, but I became unstuck and was able to get moving. I began down an entirely different discernment path that ultimately led to establishing *b*.

2. Imagine you are on your deathbed. Which choice would bring you a deep level of satisfaction, peace, even joy, as death approaches and you reflect back on your life? The use of this eternal perspective unleashes your decision from the pressures and concerns of the immediate, a pressure that can be experienced as a paralyzing weight. By enlarging one's perspective to include the eternal, the perceived magnitude of the decision will likely be significantly reduced, which in turn provides the internal space and time to more fully open to God.

3. Imagine you are with Jesus on the Day of Judgment, talking with him about the decision for which you are currently seeking confirmation. When I first came across this suggestion, I did not like it at all, but the original fear of condemnation *("day of judgment")* has been replaced over the years with encouragement, because I have come to see this more about a personal encounter with Jesus, who judges me not punitively, but who will speak the truth about my life, and who will, by his power and grace, make everything—my life included—come out right in the end. As you share your decision with Jesus, pay attention to your feelings. Are you experiencing joy, excitement, happiness, worry, concern, guilt, shame? Once again, this process helps put the decision in a larger perspective, and potentially frees you from the demands and pressure of your current circumstances.

There is a fourth suggestion that is not found in Ignatius' *Spiritual Exercises*, but was also developed by Ignatius and appears in some of his other writings. Many, myself included, have found this imaginative method quite helpful as a way of bringing to the surface the feelings surrounding a particular decision, and then helping to discern God's leading.

4. Imagine you are embracing one of the alternatives as your final choice (like moving to a new place). Then sit with your decision as if you had made it (you *are* moving), paying attention to what is going on within you, noting consolations and desolations (affect/ volitional), resistance, fears, excitement…anything stirring within you, while also opening your heart to the communications of God and the prompting of the Spirit. Stay with that alternative for a day or two, then take a break for a bit before doing the same with the other alternative (*not* moving). Once again, pay attention to what is going on within you, noticing consolations and desolations (affect/ volitional), resistance, fears, excitement…anything stirring within you, while opening your heart to the communications of God and the prompting of the Spirit. This method of imagining has helped many reach greater clarity, and even experience the inner promptings of God (Mode One or Two) that were not felt before. This is also an excellent method for couples to make use of as they decide together. They each spend time separately imagining one of the possible scenarios and then the other. When they have each finished their time in each scenario they come together and compare notes, sharing their internal experience along with any words, thoughts, or images that may have arisen during that time.

When choosing to employ imagination in your decision-making process, consider which of the above suggestions might be most helpful. As you enter into the scene, remember to pay attention to what you are feeling within; work your way all the way through the imaginative exercise, noting any words, thoughts, or images that God may be communicating with you. It is helpful to write down what you are experiencing—not judging the experiences as your write, but merely noticing them. Once you feel you have finished with the imaginative practice, prayerfully consider before God what you have felt, sensed, heard, and written down, continuing to pay attention to what is stirring within you. Did you receive a sense of confirmation to move forward, or an invitation to continue to discern or wait? Did you sense an inner movement of the Spirit (Mode One or Two)? Do you now have a fuller understanding of what God may be inviting you into? Is it in agreement with your prior decision or are you being pulled in a different direction? Remember, as you work your way through this process, you are seeking to be indifferent to all but the embodiment of God's will in ways that bring God greater honor and glory.

Finally, even after the use of your imagination and consequent time in prayer, you are instructed to offer your decision, if there is one, to God, asking God to receive and confirm or deny that your decision is indeed to God's greater service and praise. If you sensed in these uses of your imagination the confirmation you were seeking after finishing Mode Three, then implement your decision in a timely manner...always continuing to discern as you move forward.

EXERCISES:

1. What do you think are the positives and negatives of using your God-given imagination as a tool in the decision-making process?

2. Which of the suggestions for using your imagination do you think might be most helpful for you when it comes to the decision-making process?

3. How might the use of the imagination lead a person back into Mode One or Two of the Christian discernment process?

CHAPTER FIFTEEN
YOUR FOUR ACES OF CHRISTIAN DISCERNMENT

When it comes to Christian discernment, Christians may naturally feel pressure to get it right. Is God giving me freedom in this decision or do I need to hit the bullseye? Was that a drop of water hitting a rock, a sponge...or the hot dog I had for lunch? Is this really God's will for me? Because it seems too easy, too hard, too enjoyable, too different. You also know the person most easily fooled by you is yourself and, though you may seek to embrace holy indifference and desire God's will and glory above all, your motives are mixed at best. Your desires sometimes win out. UGH!

The struggle to discern correctly and then to know that you have, especially in the beginning, begs for God's help. And God faithfully provides that help in scripture, by giving you your Four Aces of power and confidence. I use the term *four aces* because of the confidence such a hand carries in poker: when you hold four aces in your hand, you gain a peaceful inner posture that enables you to be in the moment, open and responsive, to take in, appreciate, and embrace the circumstances. My hope is that the four aces of Christian discernment might reduce your stress and instill that same sense of confidence in you when you are seeking to make a big decision, or when you are forced to use Mode Three.

As you read through the four passages below, please remember these cards are always in your hand. They don't change. If you make a bad, wrong, or reckless decision, these aces are still yours to lay down again and again and again. Because God is with you, your hand is always a winning hand.

YOUR FOUR ACES

1. "...He who began a good work in you will bring it to completion..."
   –Philippians 1:6b

   As your life of Christian discernment unfolds, you never have to worry about your future. The decisions you make will not bring to an end the good work God began within you. Your salvation, your future transformation, is not up for grabs. God is faithful.

2. "And we know that for those who love God all things work together for good, for those who are called according to his purpose."
   –Romans 8:28

   God will use all your decisions, changeable and unchangeable, for your ongoing growth and development. There is nothing you can do to prevent God from bringing good out of the raw materials of your choices and the resulting circumstances. God can write straight using crooked lines.

3. "[Nothing] will be able to separate us from the love of God..." – Romans 8:38–39a

   There is nothing you can do, no choice you can make, that will separate you from God's one-of-a-kind, lavishly unconditional love. God loves you, likes you, and loves loving you. You cannot change that by making a boneheaded decision. Nothing, no thing, can separate you from God's love.

4. "...He [Jesus] who is in you is greater than he who is in the world."
   –1 John 4:4

   If Satan, who can and does appear as an angel of light, fools you by twisting a consolation or, through subtleties and persistent fallacies, draws you away "little by little" until he has ensnared you, Christ still wins. You are still loved by God. The future of the world is not in your hands, and Satan will never ultimately succeed.

Next time you need to make one of those big decisions, or any decision that feels big, take a deep breath and remember you are holding four aces in your hand. You have nothing to worry about. Perhaps this simple reminder will enable you to relax in God's hands and will create the internal space you need to hear the whispers and sense the promptings of the Spirit.

EXERCISES:

1. As you reflect on your four aces, what feelings concerning God arise within you? Take a moment and share these with God.

2. Which of the four aces brings you the greatest sense of joy and/or fosters a willingness to follow as God leads? What is it about that ace that is so meaningful for you?

3. Do you have trouble believing any of the aces are true? If so, share your feelings and doubts, freely and unedited, with God.

SECTION FIVE: ADDITIONAL INSIGHTS FOR CHRISTIAN DISCERNMENT

The chapters included in this section can be read in any order, as they are independent thoughts and Christian discernment learnings that aren't necessarily attached to previous chapters but have a place in the discussion. Let God lead you through this series of short chapters, taking from them any helpful insights to which you are drawn. You may wish to reorder them or skip one altogether, as the Spirit leads.

CHAPTER SIXTEEN

ADULT FAITH

For years I was a proponent of a concept called "adult faith," believing that just as children grow and become more and more independent, so we as Christians develop from children into adults and become better equipped to make decisions and live more independently. There are things we have just come to know and understand from going to church, studying the scripture, living life with Jesus. As Paul wrote when describing his own spiritual growth and development, "When I was a *child*, I spoke like a *child*, I thought like a *child*, I reasoned like a *child*. When I became a man, I gave up *child*ish ways (emphasis mine)" (1 Cor. 13:11).

Clearly there is a level of faith that could rightly be labeled "adult." But a problem arises when we seek to determine what exactly is meant by adult faith. Paul indicates that adult faith communicates, thinks, and reasons differently than child-like faith, but says little else on the topic. Then we, as we often do, run far afield with this verse and *voilà!*, a fully-formed concept of adult faith emerges—a concept for which there is not enough scriptural support.

Garry Friesen, in his book *Decision Making and the Will of God*, describes "adult" faith as follows, "New Testament believers are equipped to relate to their Father [God] on an adult level *without requiring the kind of detailed parental supervision that was appropriate to childhood*...This is demonstrated at the level of human relationships. In my own case, as I was growing up, my parents were training me so I could learn to make decisions for myself. They taught me to distinguish right from wrong; they taught me biblical values and principles that I could apply to specific decisions. *The older I became, the less they told me what to do*...In a similar manner, our Heavenly Father personally cares for his children (emphasis mine)."[1]

So adult faith involves moving from the dependency a child has on a parent for wisdom, instruction, and insight to the level of independence and personal responsibility that we believe characterizes an adult. As we grow in our faith, we become better able to make use of common sense and reason, to weigh options, and to draw upon the wisdom we have accumulated while walking with Jesus. A faith-infused life frees us from childish dependency on God so that we can walk with God in a more adult way.

I admit that I find all this talk of independence quite appealing, but I believe this reasoning leads us back to the garden of Eden—not the innocence of the garden, but to the disobedience of the garden, where once again we choose to eat of the fruit of the tree of good and evil. Somehow we think we can decide between good and evil apart from the input and wisdom of God. This version of "adult faith" is a veiled means of reasserting ourselves and choosing to ignore our limitations. It smacks of a type of hubris that assumes we are able to get to a point of knowing/wisdom that approaches a level of equality with God without an ongoing yielded-ness to God and real time dependence upon God.

Now if anyone were able arrive at such a level of independence, it would be Jesus, because Jesus was fully God and fully human. Jesus walked among us to show us the Father and also to show us what it means to be fully human, so it makes perfect sense to look at how Jesus lived in order to see what a truly adult faith looks like. This is NOT the same as asking, "what would Jesus do?", an impossible question to answer with any level of certainty, but instead is asking, "What did Jesus SAY about how he lived and ordered his life?"

When it comes to decision-making and discernment, Jesus never even hints at any level of independence, but rather demonstrates a relentless dependence on God and the need to hear and follow God's leading. At the end of his life, in the garden of Gethsemane, Jesus was not weighing pros and cons. He declared to his Father that he didn't want to do this (die on the cross), then resolved to do the will of God that had been made known to him. If anyone would have had the independent adult faith mentioned above, it would have been Jesus. But instead, in his words:

> *"I can do nothing on my own. As I hear, I judge, and my judgment is just, because I seek not my own will but the will of him who sent me." –John 5:30*

> *"For I have come down from heaven, not to do my own will but the will of him who sent me." –John 6:38*

> *"So Jesus said to them, 'When you have lifted up the Son of Man, then you will know that I am he, and that I do nothing on my own authority, but speak just as the Father taught me.'" –John 8:28*

I think we can assume Jesus possessed a mature faith, but it was not a faith characterized by independence. No, Jesus' adult faith was an *eyes-wide-open-faith* that knew the world was broken, that it was a place of tribulation, suffering, and pain. He knew that to follow God in such a world often leads to suffering, sacrifice, to a cross *and yet* he was still able/willing to say, *Yes, God's will be done*. This adult faith is not dependent on *feeling* God's presence, but is a faith that can *experience* the assurance of God's presence, caring, love, and wisdom in the midst of the perceived absence of God (*My God, my God, why have you forsaken me?*).

The adult faith of Jesus realizes the need for the wisdom from above, not of this world, a wisdom that is seen as foolishness by the people of the world.

This adult faith is a by-product of relationship, of time spent with the Tri-une God, owning, of embracing, trusting in, and relying on the truth of God's character as loving, wise, and powerful. Able to give God the benefit of doubt when circumstances tell a different story, this adult faith knows and owns the finiteness of human wisdom, perspective, and insight. This adult faith neces-sitates a daily walking with Jesus, an embracing of the words of Jesus that, "Apart from me you can do nothing; in the world you will have tribulation; you will be hated; others, even your brothers, will turn against you; blessed are you when you are persecuted, cursed...." (See John 15 and 16, Matt. 5 and 10, Luke 12, etc.) This faith sees beyond the world to the presence of God, the eternal, in whom we live, move, and have our being.

The description of adult faith as marked by independence and the suf-ficiency of accumulated wisdom and common sense is attractive, but it un-fortunately leads to separation from God, doing life on one's own terms, and looking for God's stamp of approval. The *eyes-wide-open-faith* demonstrated by Jesus leads instead to a greater dependency on God, an awareness of God, and is an invitation to life together—open, yielded, attentive, and aware. It is a faith that includes seeing the world as it is and ourselves as we are—finite, broken, in need of the wisdom that only God can bring.

EXERCISES:

1. What would it take for you to more fully embrace and live into the eyes-wide-open-faith?

2. What might you need to put into/take out of your life in order to develop the depth of relationship with God that is needed to live with God, able to say, "Not my will, but your will be done"?

3. How might your process of discernment change if you embraced your dependence on God for wisdom, insight, and understanding as you seek to embody God's will?

4. Which Mode or Modes of Christian discernment and decision-making reflect most closely reflect this eyes-wide-open-faith?

CHAPTER SEVENTEEN

EXTRAPOLATION

Extrapolation was the first BIG college word I learned that I could actually pronounce, spell, and remember the meaning of, so I am delighted to be able to use it in the context of Christian discernment. As I have walked through the discernment process with others for many years, I have noticed a definite propensity for people to extrapolate when it comes to life with God. There is a tendency to connect the dots, jump to conclusions, assume that we know what God is doing, what we need to do next, and what is going to happen now and down the road. The truth is that all this extrapolating is dangerous and it often leads us down a path that begins well but ends up far from where God intended. (This is similar to the consolations or God-honoring beginnings that later change, as we discussed in Chapter 12, e.g. my decision to go barefoot).

An example I've seen play out time and time again involves the job application process. Let's call our hypothetical job-seeker "Sally." Sally has been praying about a job, searching online and even submitting applications, when one day she reads a job description and immediately knows God wants her to apply for this job, no question about it. She feels that drop of water hitting a sponge and *knows* (Mode Two). She has not felt this sense of God's leading with any of the previous job applications, so she is very excited and acts without hesitation. As she fills out the application, she imagines herself starting this job and feels joy bubbling up within her. Her heart is filled with gratitude and she finds herself praising God for overflowing goodness and faithfulness. She sends off her completed application convinced of God's leading.

A week later, when she hears her God-provided job was filled by another candidate, she finds herself struggling. *Did I really hear from God? Did I misunderstand God's message?* Although natural, these questions are not that helpful at this juncture. Her first question should be, "What did God say to me in the beginning?" The answer to that question is, "God told me to apply for the job." So, what went wrong?

Sally went ahead, assuming God would give her the job, but that wasn't what was said. God may have told her to fill out the application, but here lies the danger of extrapolation: there was no promise of a resulting job. And it can get worse. What if Sally were offered the job? Since she is already convinced that applying for a job equals God's desire for her to take the job, she accepts without discerning. She now has a job that God didn't intend for her, regardless of her future success or failure. The good news is that God is gracious (see Chapter 15, "Your Four Aces of Christian Discernment") and will bring good out of the situation, but because she chose to connect the dots for herself, Sally's life is now on a different trajectory.

This is also played out when one extrapolates the impending and long-term results of a decision. If God leads me to pastor this church, it will thrive and grow. If I marry this person, we will have a wonderful, carefree life serving and worshipping God together. If I step out in faith as God is inviting me to do, I will be successful, things will go well for me and my family...you get the idea. This exuberant extrapolation that begins in faith can lead to doubt, to questioning that you heard from God at all, or worse, to rejecting the goodness and faithfulness of God. You may be blinded to what God is actually doing in and through you because the results of your decision are not what you thought they would or should be—even though they are results God never mentioned or intended. As you discern the invitation to faithfully follow God's leading, leave the results in God's hands and learn to trust God in the process.

IMPORTANT REMINDERS

1. Beware of the tendency to extrapolate further than the communications or promptings of the Spirit actually dictate, even though your conclusions seem logical or a matter of common sense.

2. Use the results of your God-guided decisions to lead you toward God, not away from God, even if you feel anger, frustration, or confusion.

3. Remember the aces you are forever holding when you make decisions; let them remind you of the faithfulness of God and of God's power and love.

I want to mention three other manifestations of extrapolation (quite the phrase) I have commonly seen in my journeys with others:

- "When Sabrina retires, I do not know if I want to continue to work here without her, and I certainly do not want to leave at the same time as she does or shortly afterward, as it will reflect poorly on me. I need to…"

- "If they make these decisions, I do not know if I will be able to continue to work here, as the demands and pressures will continue to grow, and I am not willing to endure the added stress. I need to…"

- "Given my current situation and the needs of this organization, I am going to be asked to do things that I do not desire to do, nor do I believe I have the gifts and abilities to fulfill the role(s) they will be asking me to take on. I need to…."

Each of the subtle forms of extrapolation listed above are being internalized in such a way that they are producing worry and uneasiness, i.e., desolation. One of the most helpful rules for decision-making I can give you is this one, which I have given you before: **Do not change a decision you made in consolation during a time of desolation**. Yet that very temptation is what each of the above individuals is facing. Each is trying to come up with a reasonable plan that makes sense given the situation. But each has fallen into the trap of extrapolation—projecting perceived future outcomes based on what they now think they know and feel. When God communicates to you or when you sense the promptings of the Spirit, heed the words of Mary to the servants in John 2, and "Do whatever he tells you" —no more and no less.

Jesus has an important message for us when facing an unknown future, "Therefore do not be anxious about tomorrow, for tomorrow will be anxious for itself. Sufficient for the DAY is its own trouble (emphasis mine)" (Matt. 6:34). When we extrapolate, we are guessing about future events while projecting on the future our current concerns and feelings. Instead, by turning to God in the moment, desolation becomes volitional consolation, and we become more aware of God's presence with us—loving, leading, and guiding, one day at a time.

EXERCISES:

1. Why do you think people are so quick to extrapolate? Is this something you find yourself doing? If so, why? If not, how do you avoid it?

2. Do you have a tendency to judge the rightness or wrongness of the decisions you make based on their perceived and immediate results? How might that keep you from experiencing God in those very realities? How might the truth that God is above all we can think, ask or imagine enable us to view results differently and, in turn, open to God in all circumstances?

Chapter Eighteen

Community and Christian Discernment

As Christians we are part of a community called the Church, which transcends time and space and is also localized in time and space. We are surrounded by a crowd of witnesses who have gone before us, and we are also a part of an eternal community called the Trinity who journey with us, even within us. Ours is a communal existence, united by the Spirit; we are sisters and brothers in Christ who are invited to do life together.

Community was very real for the early church, as Paul emphasizes over and over again in his writings: it's seen in his image of the body of Christ (1 Cor. 12), in his declaration that God has destroyed the barrier, the dividing wall of hostility (Eph. 2:14) between people groups, in the removal of distinctions such as Jew and Greek, slave and free, male and female, in his clear proclamation that all are one in Christ (Gal. 3:25). So it is not surprising that communal discernment was a necessary process in the early church (Acts 13, 15).

It is exciting for me to see that once again there is a growing interest in communal discernment—groups gathering together to listen for God's wisdom. This has been faithfully practiced in different Christian groups for centuries, but now books and articles are being written and seminars are being offered dealing with the nuts and bolts of communal discernment. All this attention is very helpful, informative, and needed, but I fear we are trying to run before we have learned to walk.

The writer of Hebrews articulates a reality regarding discernment that I believe exists today. Hebrew 5:12–14 states, "For though by this time you ought to be teachers, you need someone to teach you again the basic principles of the oracles of God. You need milk, not solid food, for everyone who lives on milk is unskilled in the word of righteousness, since he is a child. But solid food is for the mature, for those who have their powers of discernment trained by constant practice to distinguish good from evil." The writer is alarmed at the low level of the spiritual maturity of his readers. They have not even trained themselves to discern good from evil, so how could they be expected to discern the best from the good, or recognize the devil appearing as an angel of light?

Ruth Haley Barton, in her book *Pursuing God's Will Together*, affirms the current inadequacy within the church when it comes to communal discernment simply by the way she structures her pages. She wisely spends the first 165 of her 232 pages providing insights, wisdom, and exercises designed to help form and shape leadership teams so they are spiritually ready to discern together. This is quite telling; communal discernment doesn't just happen as a result of gathering together and following a comprehensive strategy for decision-making. No, communal discernment flows from communities of people who have personally cultivated a practiced way of life that fosters their ability to be aware and indifferent, to recognize the communications of God in expected and unexpected places, and to distinguish good from evil and perceive what is best. Then and only then are they able to discern God's will together as a community. Christians who are not living discerning lives are ill equipped to enter into communal discernment free from the influential forces of common sense, the inherent values of the culture, and the siren call of success.

I believe communal discernment can be very helpful and there are many good models available, but you need to pay special attention to the individuals you choose to be a part your communal discernment group. Each needs to be living a life led by the Spirit, seeking to embody God's will and live Jesus. There is a huge difference between a group of people who care about you and want the best for you, and a group of people who gather to listen with you, asking questions and seeking to help discern God's will for your life. Putting together such a group and then listening to its counsel may involve unpopular choices or a course that appears unwise, but the discernment of such a group can be trusted when it's comprised of Christians who live discerning lives who gather to listen for the whispers of God.

A key element of communal discernment is indifference to everything but God's leading. When people know us and care about us, it can be difficult for them to be indifferent. I am often invited to journey with people who are in the process of discerning but there are times I've had to decline because I knew it would be extremely difficult for me to remain indifferent. My personal desire to continue in relationship and intimate knowledge of their circumstances overrides my ability to be free to listen for God's wisdom. Be aware of such inclinations in your own heart, and be wise about the groups you join.

SEEKING WISE COUNSEL

Where does seeking the wisdom of others fit into the discernment process? The Bible strongly encourages us to seek advice from those who have been on the journey longer, who are practitioners in a field of interest, or who are working in the line of work to which you feel drawn (e.g., the long-married, parents of children older than your own, etc.). It is good to seek out the help of those who are a bit ahead of you—or way ahead—when it comes to looking for those who will understand your circumstances and be helpful in guiding you onward.

> *Where there is no guidance, a people falls, but in an abundance of counselors there is safety.* –Proverbs 11:14

The way of a fool is right in his own eyes, but a wise man listens to advice. –Proverbs 12:15

Without counsel plans fail, but with many advisers they succeed. –Proverbs 15:22

The accumulating of wisdom from others is a good thing, but it is not without its own set of pitfalls and concerns. It is important to prayerfully discern what you are hearing and to continue to reflect on what you have heard, listening for the Spirit, and for the inner communications of God in and through what was shared.

One danger inherent in the counsel of others—learning from the acquired wisdom and practical insights developed over time by individuals—is that such wisdom is often rooted and grounded in a particular setting or situation and needs to be contextualized for the current realities and circumstances. People also bring their own baggage along with their experiences, and not all of that baggage is helpful. It's important to glean principles from what wise counselors share and then seek to contextualize them in your own setting, while always remaining sensitive to God's subtle nudging.

When you are willing to seek and listen to wise counsel, you are embracing the best possible inner posture for hearing from God. You are admitting your need and desire for wisdom; you are open (indifferent) to hearing what others have to share. It is this humility and openness of heart that will serve you well as you journey in this way. As you listen to wise counselors, be aware of the quickening of your spirit that tells you that what was spoken is more than a person's experience or insights, but that God is in those words. Remember those "God words" and process them later in conversation with God.

This inward posture of heart opens you to seeing and hearing from God not only in conversations with others, but through creation, circumstances, scripture, songs, or a passing comment. This is what is meant by having ears to hear, a way of life that is desirous of, open to, and continually asking for the wisdom of God (James 1:5). Ask for wisdom and God will provide.

Here too is where spiritual direction can be of help. A spiritual director is one gifted from God and trained to come alongside others in ways that help them to listen to God, and to begin to become aware of how God may be communicating, guiding, and prompting them. A spiritual director keeps a healthy indifference that can help you reflect and listen, to open to God and courageously enter where God may be inviting you—even if it isn't the easy way or the way that is culturally accepted.

In Christ, we are part of a great and gifted community; and living in community, we are called and instructed to avail ourselves of the many resources God provides through communal discernment, wise counsel, and spiritual direction, always listening for the communications of God and the promptings of the Spirit.

> ## EXERCISES:
>
> *1. Who are spiritually mature people in your life who can help you listen to the communications of God?*
>
> *2. Who are those individuals who are able to be indifferent as they listen to and with you, desiring God's will be done in and through you no matter what?*

CHAPTER NINETEEN

DESIRE AND MOTIVATION

Given our emphasis on the importance of holy indifference, you might be surprised to find a chapter entitled "Desire and Motivation." But desires and holy indifference are companions, not enemies. Holy indifference does not mean emptying yourself of all desires. Instead, it offers a freedom from misaligned and disordered desires, and in their place, it gives us the ability to desire that which is most desirable: God and the fullness of life God has made available. Holy indifference allows godly desires to grow and fuel your life with God.

C.S. Lewis has a lovely comment on Christians and desires: "It would seem that our Lord finds our desires not too strong, but too weak. We are half hearted creatures, fooling about with drink and sex and ambition when infinite joy is offered us, like an ignorant child who wants to go on making mud pies in the slum because she cannot imagine what is meant by the offer of a holiday at the sea. We are far too easily pleased."[1]

In the Psalms we see how one's desire for God leads to a valuing of one's relationship with God and the subsequent ordering of one's life to fulfill those deep desires:

- "O God, you are my God; earnestly I seek you; my soul thirsts for you; my flesh faints for you, as in a dry and weary land where there is no water. So I have looked upon you in the sanctuary, beholding your power and glory. Because your steadfast love is better than life, my lips will praise you." –Psalm 63:1–3

- "Whom have I in heaven but you? And there is nothing on earth that I desire besides you. My flesh and my heart may fail, but God is the strength of my heart and my portion forever…But for me it is good to be near God; I have made the Lord God my refuge…" –Psalm 73:25–26, 28a

- "As a deer pants for flowing streams, so pants my soul for you, O God. My soul thirsts for God, for the living God…" –Psalm 42:1–2a

St Augustine put it this way: "The whole life of the good Christian is a holy longing."[2] And Thomas Merton wrote, "Life is shaped by the end you live for. You are made in the image of what you desire."[3]

As your desires for God and for the life that is yours in Christ grow, you are more apt to resist the cotton-candy pleasures the world so readily offers, pleasures that ruin your appetite for the deeper desires that flow from being in relationship with God.

Some with whom I journey, who outwardly express a desire to know and embody God's will, have hearts that tell a different tale. In the words of Paul, "For they all seek their *own interests*, not those of Jesus Christ (emphasis mine)" (Phil. 2:21). They might come seeking God's will, but with a number of stipulations that God must meet if they are to be willing to follow: a bigger house, financial security, a smaller city, a larger city, nearness to family, good schools… Or they come in the midst of a time of desolation, seeking to escape a challenging situation, to get themselves out of trouble or to pursue that which they believe will be the source of happiness. Their primary concerns are not really to know and embody God's will.

When our desires are not purified by holy indifference, we are unable to make decisions motivated by a desire to honor God, and the wisdom from God we are seeking is not forthcoming. As James clearly states, "When you ask, you do not receive, because you ask with wrong motives, that you may spend what you get on your pleasures" (James 4:3 NIV). Having a conflicted heart blocks access to the wisdom and resources critical to Christian discernment. Believing that the problem lies with God and not within ourselves, we are forced to use the only tools at our disposal and, imprisoned in the two dimensional world of intellect and common sense, to make critical decisions in the worst circumstances (time of desolation).

DESIRES AND DISCERNMENT

In order to practice Christian discernment (Modes One and Two), it is critical that we are aware of our desires and where they lead; are they taking us to God (volitional consolation) or from God (volitional desolation)? If our hearts desire God above all, we are in a place of access to all the resources God provides for Christian discernment. If our hearts are conflicted and our desires lead us away from God, we are in a time of desolation and have no business making a decision at all.

Robert Jonas and Wilkie Au comment on the importance of one's desires for God when it comes to one's ability to exercise Christian discernment:

> *"Sound spiritual (Christian) discernment requires acknowledging that the root longing of our soul is for God, who alone can satisfy our heart's deepest yearning" (Au).*[4]

> *"[Christian] discernment is an inner listening and responding to that place within us where our deepest desires align with God's desire" (Jonas).*[5]

There are three important questions when it comes to understanding Christian discernment and desires:

- Am I willing to admit my need for God's wisdom and leading while still desiring (or at the very least, desiring the desire) to follow as God leads me?

- Do I truly desire to hear the communications of God, even if it means I would need to suspend my plans—move from a place of comfort and safety, leave my security, turn away from what I have built and established, leave family and friends, be thought of as foolish, irresponsible (holy indifference), etc.?

- Do I desire to submit my will to God's, in order to choose that which glorifies and honors God, to be the flesh through which God's desires are lived?

The problem often is not that I am resistant to obeying God's will as it is revealed to me. The real struggle occurs when I do NOT desire to seek God's will regarding certain matters—not necessarily the so-called the big decisions of life, but those smaller everyday decisions that mold and shape me over time. I can rationalize it, telling myself that God doesn't care about the little things so why even ask, when what is actually going on is that I desire to maintain control regarding eating, watching television, how I use my time, and how I spend my money. I feel well-equipped to captain my life without interference from God in my day-to-day life. I am not talking about choosing evil over good, but about those things that are lawful and permissible, but possibly not profitable or beneficial (see 1 Cor. 6:12, 10:23 NIV). These indulgent desires sabotage my ability to discern, and I end up settling for mud pies because I am unwilling to connect with the deeper desire of my heart. My deepest desire is to know and love God, serve others, and experience the fullness of life that is mine in and through Christ…and this is God's deepest desire for me as well.

EXERCISES:

1. Which of the three questions listed above tends to be the most difficult one for you to say yes to? Why?

2. Reflect on the C.S. Lewis quote, "It would seem that our Lord finds our desires not too strong, but too weak. We are half hearted creatures, fooling about with drink and sex and ambition when infinite joy is offered us, like an ignorant child who wants to go on making mud pies in the slum because she cannot imagine what is meant by the offer of a holiday at the sea. We are far too easily pleased." As you reflect on the level of your desire to follow God, do you see yourself as more of a mud-pie person or a holiday-at-the-beach person? Why?

CHAPTER TWENTY

HEART AND HEAD

Once upon a time, the head (thinking/reason/objective truth) and heart (feelings/emotions/desires/subjective truth) were fast friends. They were inseparable and would be seen everywhere together: at dances, at scholarly debates, and especially at church. They fed off one another, each the better for the other's presence. Great thoughts about God fanned the flame of love for God in the heart, leading to greater thoughts about God.

The scriptures (Old and New Testament) link heart and mind, even at times using them as synonyms. The writer of Hebrews, referring to the power of the living words of scripture, writes of its ability to discern thoughts and intentions of the heart (Hebrews 4:12) and Jesus states, "Love the Lord your God with all your heart and with all your soul and with all your mind" (Matt. 22:37). The mind and heart are to be companions living in harmony with one another, each informing and shaping the other; joined, not separated.

But times changed, and in those changing times, the popularity of the head grew, beginning with the rise of Scholasticism (11th–12th centuries).

It was subtle at first. The head and heart still went to each other's homes and attended the same parties and events, but the heart was becoming more of a B-list guest and the head rose to become a regular on the A-list. In fact on a number of occasions, the heart was belittled and marginalized. This trend intensified in the Age of Enlightenment (17th–18th centuries), when the heart was no longer even on the B-list. If the head was invited to a party, it was certain that the heart would not be on the guest list at all. This trend, at least in part, found its way into the church, where heart and emotions became suspect, distrusted, and at times ushered out.

This unfortunate division remains alive and well today, as the tendency within the western church is to encourage the use of the mind, almost to the exclusion of the heart, as the only valid source of knowledge. Knowledge must be quantifiable and anything that even hints of subjectivity is viewed with suspicion; this point of view has huge implications for Christian discernment and the role of the Spirit.

Yet the Triune God we follow does not always make sense to us, often defies logic and common sense. God and the ways of God are incapable of being fully comprehended intellectually. The truth is that we cannot truly know God without the heart, for knowing God flows out of relationship with God. One of the words for *to know* in Hebrew (and also in Greek) denotes an experiential aspect to knowing. If we seek to discern God's leading with head alone, to solely employ reason, common sense, and logic, our ability to discern is inadequate at best.

God's ways are not always reasonable to us, and so without heart, we are hard-pressed to see God's ways as anything but foolish. Heart is a significant part of life with God in general and particularly in the decision-making process. God does not often make sense in the bottom-line, pragmatic, production-orientated, reason-driven, success-worshipping world.

Oswald Chambers writes, "Never let your common sense become so prominent and forceful that it pushes the Son of God to one side. Common sense is a gift that God gave to our human nature—but common sense is not the gift of His Son. Supernatural sense is the gift of His Son, and we should never put our common sense on the throne. The Son always recognizes and identifies with the Father, but common sense has never yet done so and never will."[1]

Gordon T. Smith reminds us, "We must listen with heart and mind."[2] And David Benner states, "Tending to not know or trust feelings, people who live predominantly in thoughts and rational analysis need to learn to embrace their feelings. Doing so is a way of becoming more fully alive and fully human.

Such people—and I count myself among them—have forgotten how to experience the world through feelings. Feelings bring new data that is missing when only thoughts are trusted."[3]

The coming of the Holy Spirit makes it possible for us to reconcile heart and head. Through the Spirit, that which was once viewed as the foolishness of God

> 66 *Trust in the Lord with all your heart and lean not on your own understanding; in all your ways submit to him, and he will make your paths straight.* 99 *(Prov. 3:5–6).*

can be seen as the wisdom of God; the ways and thoughts of God are now available to us. Through the Spirit, we are able to factor Jesus into the equation of decision-making, and that is another game changer.

Including Jesus in the equations of Christian discernment and decision-making shatters the limiting $2 + 2 = 4$ way of looking at the world. The life of Jesus frees us from the seemingly irresistible gravitational pull of logic and reason and the confines of what we can taste, see, and touch. We are now open to the often-confounding wisdom from above, a wisdom that can run counter to reason, logic, and common sense. Check the equations below:

- 6 empty stone pots + 120 gallons of water + **Jesus** = fine-quality wine for an entire wedding party (John 2:1–12).

- 2 fish + 5 loaves of bread + **Jesus** = a catered meal for 5,000 people (Matthew 14:13–21).

- 1 paralytic + 3 friends + 1 hole in a roof + **Jesus** = 1 person walking out the front door, forgiven and healed, mat in hand (Mark 2:1–12).

- 1 crown of thorns + 2 wooden crossbeams + 3 nails + 1 spear + 1 empty tomb + **Jesus** = love, grace, forgiveness, transformation, and freedom available to all (John 19:1–20:10).

As we re-engage our heart and make room for the **faith-infused mathematics** of Christian discernment, we can begin to appreciate Blaise Pascal's words, "The heart has reasons that reason knows not."[4]

EXERCISES:

1. How have you seen and experienced Jesus turning the 2 + 2 = 4 common-sense way of looking at the world upside-down? Take some time to construct some additional mathematics of faith from your own life.

2. How do you feel about the need to pay attention to your heart as you seek to embody God's will? What would it look like for your heart and head to work together as you seek to follow the leading of the Spirit? What might keep you from allowing your heart to play a more significant role as you discern?

3. In 1 Corinthians 2:15 Paul tells us, "for the foolishness of God is wiser than human wisdom." How does his statement speak to the danger of depending primarily on human wisdom when discerning God's will?

CHAPTER TWENTY-ONE

MAKING GOD LAUGH

Whattt place does planning have in the *life of discernment* you ask? As we think about reorienting our lives to be more dependent on God, planning has to be part of the conversation. Most of us have electronic calendars on multiple devices to help us keep track of our myriad of plans so that they do not start conflicting with one another. Plans are a part of normal life, but are they part of a life of Christian discernment?

I have always enjoyed the tongue-in-cheek question and answer in the box below. As a father, it brought to mind the plans my children would dream up, many of which drew a smile and a few that gave me pause. But I also think of my heavenly Father looking at my plans and smiling. I think my idyllic way of understanding this saying filtered my reading of the passage in James 4:13–16 that talks about making your plans

> Question: *How do you make God laugh?*
>
> Answer: *Tell God your plans.*

and then adding, "If the Lord will." I took that verse as a kind of tip of my cap to God, as if to say, "Yes God, I am making some plans, but just let me know if you have something else in mind." To be truthful, I never expected God to change my plans, nor did I intentionally check in with God regarding them.

My perspective on this passage changed one day in church. As it was read aloud, I could not believe what I was hearing. I actually read it again, right there in the service, in a couple of translations, because what I heard was so drastically different than my previous understanding. The God presented in this passage was not smiling when I talked of my plans.

"Now listen, you who say, 'Today or tomorrow we will go to this or that city, spend a year there, carry on business and make money.' Why, you do not even know what will happen tomorrow. What is your life? You are a mist that appears for a little while and then vanishes. Instead, you ought to say, 'If it is the Lord's will, we will live and do this or that.' As it is, you boast in your arrogant schemes. All such boasting is evil" (James 4:13–16).

And *The Message* puts it this way, "And now I have a word for you who brashly announce, 'Today—at the latest, tomorrow—we're off to such and such a city for the year. We're going to start a business and make a lot of money.' You don't know the first thing about tomorrow. You're nothing but a wisp of fog, catching a brief bit of sun before disappearing. Instead, make it a habit to say, 'If the Master wills it and we're still alive, we'll do this or that.' As it is, you are full of your grandiose selves" (James 4:13–16).

This time through the passage, I heard God saying, "Who do you think you are to make plans—what do you know, how long are you even going to be around?" This version is a far cry from what I previously thought was being communicated. But it makes so much more sense! The life of Christian discernment we are invited to live is a life with God of dependence and yieldedness. It is the life Jesus lived, a life of submission, following as the Spirit led, speaking and doing as the Father desired—the very life Jesus made possible for us to live through his death, resurrection, and gift of the Holy Spirit.

Making plans gives us a sense that we are captains of our own destiny, which is exactly what James is speaking against. He reminds us that we are finite, as sturdy and long-lasting as the fog. So when it comes to making plans, we need to be very careful, to check our attitudes and embrace humility. As we look at Paul's life, we see an obvious necessity for plans, IF they are made with a deep awareness of where we are on the planning pecking order. Here are some examples from the epistles:

- "But on taking leave of them [Paul] said, 'I will return to you if God wills,' and he set sail from Ephesus" (Acts 18:21).

- "But I will come to you soon, if the Lord wills..." (1 Cor. 4:19).

- "For I do not want to see you now just in passing. I hope to spend some time with you, if the Lord permits" (1 Cor. 16:7).

And the writer of Hebrews shows the same attitude: "And this we will do, if God permits" (Heb. 6:3).

In each of the above passages, plans and desires are genuinely and humbly released to God. This attitude of humility is entirely different than the off-handed gestures of submission I made earlier in my life.

The danger lies in not including God's ongoing wisdom and input throughout the planning process and beyond. It is so easy to embrace a good and worthy goal, become convinced that it's what God wants, and then come up with a plan to do everything in our power to make it happen. We no longer discern, no longer pay attention to the communications of God or the promptings of the Spirit. On autopilot, we may accomplish what we have set out to do, but we also may very well discover that over time the initial good and holy thoughts have become less so, landing us far from where God wanted us to be or even where we originally intended—at least internally.

Plans need to be held in open hands. Read the following verses that talk about the interplay between God and humans when it comes to plans:

- "The plans of the heart belong to man, but the answer of the tongue is from the Lord" (Prov. 16:1).

- "The heart of man plans his way, but the Lord establishes his steps" (Prov. 16:9).

- "The lot is cast into the lap. But its every decision is from the Lord" (Prov. 16:33).

- "Many are the plans in the mind of a man, but it is the purpose of the Lord that will stand" (Prov. 19:21).

- "A man's steps are from the Lord; how then can man understand his way?" (Prov. 20:24).

This admonishment actually pertains to all plans *and all changes in plans*: an unexpected layover, more traffic than you anticipated, a longer line at the grocery store. Any and all changes in the events you had planned can now be viewed as invitations from God to be open to what God may have for you in these moments.

Paradoxically, plans can hinder our ability to discern unless we choose to hold them in w-i-d-e open hands before God, aware of and alert to the whispers of God and the promptings of the Spirit.

Often when it comes to the will of God, we desire a road map and, if God doesn't give us one, we create our own, ordering our lives in a direction that will get us where we want to go. God does not give us road maps, but a GPS (*God Provided Spirit*, see Chapter 23) to guide and direct. Using that GPS requires humility, trust, dependency, and a willingness to follow as God makes known the next steps.

EXERCISES:

1. Why are people so inclined to make plans? What are the possible pitfalls of making plans?

2. When making plans, what can you do to help you hold your plans loosely, so you can continue to be open to the leading of the Spirit?

DAILY PRACTICE:

I am not going to ask you to stop making plans, but I am going to invite you to intentionally turn to God when your plans do not go the way you intended. If an appointment is canceled, instead of immediately coming up with another plan, try to see it as an opportunity to turn your attention to God; be open to the prompting of the Spirit and see if God will now direct you. I have experienced some amazing "divine appointments" that would never had happened if my plans had not fallen through. You can trust God to make the most of unexpected opportunities.

CHAPTER TWENTY-TWO

TIMELY OBEDIENCE, CIRCUMSTANCES, OPEN DOORS

Christian discernment is not about gathering data or acquiring spiritual wisdom, but gaining clarity in order to embody God's will in action. After we hear and recognize the communications of God and sense the prompting of the Spirit, it's time to obediently act. We see this in Acts 13:2–3: "While they were worshiping the Lord and fasting, the Holy Spirit said, 'Set apart for me Barnabas and Saul for the work to which I have called them.' Then after fasting and praying they laid their hands on them and sent them off." Discernment of the Spirit by the apostles led to immediate, obedient action.

One Old Testament story illustrates the need to act in a timely manner when we are aware of God's leading. In Numbers 13 and 14, twelve spies were sent to explore the land of Canaan, the land God was giving to Israel. When the spies returned, ten of the twelve shared what they saw and experienced and urged the community to disobey God and not enter the Promised land for they thought it was too dangerous to do so. The other two urged the people to obey God and enter the land, not refuting the experience of the ten, but pointing to God's faithfulness (*eyes-wide-open-faith*). But the ten prevailed, and the community refused to enter the land. In turn, God rescinded the offer, informing the Israelites that because this generation chose to disobey, they would never enter the promised land, but that that privilege would be granted their children. And there's more…the next morning, the people, admitting they had sinned, were ready to go in and claim the land. But Moses said, *No, it is too late, you had your chance. If you go now, you will be disobeying God again and will not be victorious.* It's a harsh truth, but once we have discerned God's leading (it was clear that God wanted them to enter the land), it is time to act regardless of our fears or reservations. Inactivity can cause us to miss out on God's adventure altogether.

Timeliness does not necessarily mean in the next hour, day, week, or even year. Timeliness is about beginning, taking that first step, getting started—whatever that may entail. Those people in the above story simply needed to begin in obedience and trust; the actual taking and settling of the land was going to take some time. *Timely obedience is moving in the direction God has made clear to you when God makes it clear—even if that movement is only a baby step.*

CIRCUMSTANCES AND OPEN DOORS

When I began this book I felt much differently about "circumstances" than I do now. Although I hadn't spent much time thinking about the connection between discernment and circumstances, I accepted the view held by people a lot smarter than I am, which is to say that circumstances play an important role in Christian discernment. But, while admitting I would rather have favorable circumstances than unfavorable circumstances when seeking to live into God's leading, I now believe circumstances, good or bad, are neither an aid to discernment nor an indication (and certainly not a sign) that I have or have not discerned correctly. God can use circumstances and communicate through them, but circumstances have no authority in and of themselves and are not to be used to sway or dissuade you from following what you have come to realize is God's leading. The Lord spoke or prompted, and now you need to get moving regardless, and possibly in spite of, the circumstances—this is timely obedience.

But having said that, I need to differentiate between general circumstances and the more specific occasions when we experience something and instantly know God is involved. These God-infused circumstances are significantly different than ordinary circumstances in that the Spirit is making known to us a spiritual reality that transcends the visible. We are able to sense, see, and know the invisible, the eternal. While a true gift, this spiritual happening alone is not confirmation of God's leading. Remember the earlier discussion about Satan appearing as an angel of light (Chapter 12), that he is able to use even good and holy thoughts for his twisted purposes. Seeing God at work is an invitation to discern if in fact God is inviting one to join in that particular work, but not a confirmation in and of itself.

This ambiguity is also true in the case of open doors. Just because a door is open does not mean we are to go through it. I may stick my head through, trying to discern if God is leading me further, but—just as in seeing God at work in circumstances—an open door needs further discernment. Now, if we are living a lifestyle of discernment, open to God and the Spirit, desiring to do God's will above all, we may very well experience the *Spirit-infused-spontaneous-incisiveness* that knows in the moment whether or not to pass through the open door. A discerning life is often privy to God's thoughts and wisdom in real time.

YES AND NO

In Acts 16, we see the Holy Spirit preventing Paul from preaching the word in the province of Asia. The door was open, but the Holy Spirit said no! Later, in Acts 16:9–10, Paul is given a vision and instantly knows he is being called to preach the gospel in Macedonia. The previous "no" from the Spirit freed Paul for assignment,

> *When dealing with others it is always easier to change a no to a yes than to turn a yes into no.*

to embrace this new opportunity to embody God's will. It is important to discern our yes's and no's, as every yes is also a no to something we don't yet know and every no opens up opportunities to say yes in the future. Since we do not know what the future holds, it is exceedingly important to seek God's wisdom and guidance regarding our yes's and no's.

THERE IS A RISK

While waiting for favorable circumstance or an open door *could* be born out of a desire to make sure we heard correctly—which is quite understandable—it may also be a ploy we use to avoid immediate action. Know that it is entirely possible to feel fear around moving forward once God has spoken because there is no guarantee of success. We have no idea what will follow, but that isn't our concern. God calls us to be faithful. Even Christian discernment always involves risk. We do not know where our actions will lead, but we do know God is with us, and nothing will separate us from God's love (and the other three aces—see Chapter 15). The goal of Christian discernment is faithful obedience in a timely manner.

Note: Two additional enemies of timely obedience are procrastination and perfectionism. As I dragged my feet far too long before beginning this book, I realized that my procrastination was simply disobedience made presentable. Once I started calling procrastinating what it really was, disobedience, I was able to start and continue writing. I do not have personal experience with perfectionism, but I have seen how waiting to be fully prepared or perfectly right can negatively affect a person's forward movement or can prompt the perfectionist to immediately act as a reaction to a fear of failure—choosing to dive into something head-first rather than taking the time to discern. In either case, perfectionism is disobedience dressed up in a much nicer outfit than procrastination, but it is still disobedience. Call these traits what they are and ask God for help moving forward; no need to die in the desert when the ⁀ed land is so close.

EXERCISES:

1. What role do you think circumstances and open doors play in the discernment process? Do you agree or disagree with my view?

2. Are there any current yes's in your life that God may want to turn into a no? Are there any no's that you may need to revisit and possibly change to a yes? Ask God to help you think through your yes's and no's in order to discover if the changeable decisions should be changed.

3. Is there something God wants you to do that you have not yet done? Prayerfully revisit the situation, asking God to help you discover what is hindering your obedience and what it would look like to move forward.

CHAPTER TWENTY-THREE

GPS AND CHRISTIAN DISCERNMENT

God has provided the Spirit to guide and direct us, to make the words, thoughts, insights and wisdom of God known to us, so that we can be led by the Spirit and embody God's will. In the New Testament, Paul is unable to even conceive of a Christian who is not being led by God's Provided Spirit, yet most of us are still waiting for a map of the route we will be traveling, and we are not desiring—much less relying on—our spiritual GPS.

Instead of a GPS, we prefer the map spread out on our dining room table, so we can look it over as we sip our coffee, evaluating the prescribed route and coming up with alternatives, short cuts, or some exciting, fun-filled side trips along the way. The map invites us to suppose that we are collaborators who can provide a supposed improvement on God's suggested course. Yes, a map gives us a level of control, the comfort of knowing our route ahead of time, but God is no mapmaker.

Instead of a map, we are given the Spirit, God's GPS, who guides and directs us, turn by turn fostering a dependence that makes many uncomfortable. This is a real-time dependence that necessitates an ongoing listening and responsiveness to the leading of the Spirit moment by moment. Our spiritual

GPS is not a device, but is much *better* than a device: our GPS is a personal guide who is on the path with us and who knows us, loves us, and calls us by name. Our personal GPS invites us to follow the path uniquely, independently chosen for us.

LESSONS FROM THE GPS

Let's take a few moments to compare and contrast an ordinary, physical GPS and **God's Provided Spirit**.

Each one provides information, as it is needed. Whereas your GPS provides an audible voice, God's Provided Spirit is often experienced as an inner prompting—a drop of water gently landing on a sponge or hitting a rock—that leads to a deep knowledge of the correct path ahead.

Each one provides course corrections when you make a wrong turn. I could swear that my GPS voice sounds irritated when I make a wrong move, but there is no condemnation from God's Provided Spirit. In fact, God can and does bring good out of life's wrong turns, whether made willfully or accidentally.

The GPS does not always offer the shortest route nor the quickest way. This is true of God's Provided Spirit too. God's ways are not always the shortest or fastest because God's goal is not that you simply arrive at a location. God is using the journey to mold and shape you, assuring that the person who arrives is different than the one who began the journey and is ready for the new invitations and challenges awaiting.

At times it seems that the GPS is giving new instructions every few feet: Turn right; turn left, take the first right at the roundabout. Such a rapid-fire flurry of information is not often our experience with God's Provided Spirit, but it is important to be aware and listening just in case there may be a series of turns up ahead; be ready for God's Spirit-infused-spontaneous-incisiveness.

On a recent road trip to Colorado, my wife and I were on a highway designated by our GPS, which instructed us to take a right turn in 351 miles. At times God's Provided Spirit will give clear direction as well, and though you may not be told exactly how long you will be on a path, you sense it will be a very long time.

Sometimes the GPS in our car suddenly comes up with a new direction that is inconsistent with the previous one. If you have experienced this malfunction, you know to just keep on going, as there is a glitch and the new information is faulty. This too can happen with God's Provided Spirit, although not because of a glitch with God. More than likely it's the enemy or our own desires to experience something new. We think we receive a new direction from God.

I have experienced this directional change regarding b, the spiritual formation ministry I started in 2005. Although God has made our organizational path perfectly clear for over eleven years, every so often in an effort to help someone or meet a need, or to say yes because I want to, I veer from the path. Although God is gracious and uses it for good, I have paid a price each time. If God has you on a particular path for a long period of time, it is important to continue to listen, as decisions are changeable. But if you believe you are hearing new directions from God's Provided Spirit, directions that seem contrary to the original ones, take time to discern if these are truly from God. If you are unsure, continue on the original path until you are certain. This advice also applies when you think you lose "the signal." Keep going in the last known direction until God's Provided Spirit is "back online"—when you are once again hearing the Spirit, recognizing the communications of God.

Again, God is not a mapmaker, but has given us the Spirit to guide and direct us. The key is to be listening and responsive to God's Provided Spirit. Just as Jesus was led by the Spirit and thus dependent on the Spirit, you are called to live the same open, yielded, and obedient life. As you follow God's Provided Spirit, you may not take the fastest or the shortest route, but know for certain that the route God gives you will help you to know and experience God, be used by God and transformed along the way into more of the person God has created and called you to be.

EXERCISES:

1. Why might people desire a map from God rather than the GPS God has provided?

2. What are the invitations, challenges, and advantages that accompany a relational, God-given GPS?

Appendix

RECOLLECTION

This prayer provides a way to name and embrace our unshakable identity in Christ, and fosters trust in and dependence on God. As we consistently practice this prayer, internalizing our identity in Christ more deeply, we are free to be more fully who God has called and created us to be, and to follow where Jesus leads. It is called the "prayer of recollection" because it involves an intentional remembering of who we are as God's new creation; we are reminded that apart from Christ we can do nothing. As we consistently pray this prayer, we will come to embrace these truths at deeper and deeper levels.

The first part of the prayer helps us to name and own our limitations as a finite person, while also affirming that this is not the end of the story. In the second part of the prayer, we recall to mind, heart, and soul who we are in Christ. Finally, we reflect on and savor the love God lavishes upon us.

THE THREE AFFIRMATIONS OF RECOLLECTION:

1. "I am a finite person. Apart from Christ I can do nothing and God's grace/strength is manifested in my weakness. I can do all in and through Christ Jesus who strengthens me." (2 Cor. 12:9, John 15:5, Phil 4:13)

2. "I name, embrace and celebrate my soul's true identity as a person who is…"

   - Forgiven (Colossians 1:13–14, Matthew 26:27–28, Ephesians 1:7–8)

- Justified (Romans 5:1–11)

- Sanctified (Romans 6:1–14)

- Adopted (Romans 8:15–17a, Ephesians 1:5)

- Belonging to God (Romans 14:7–8, 1 Peter 2:9)

- Containing God (1 Corinthians 3:16, Galatians 2:20)

- Beloved of God (Colossians 3:12)

Instead of praying through the entirety of the above list, you could choose one identifier to focus on each day. If you do, please endeavor to keep it in your heart and mind throughout your day, helping you remember and own your unchangeable identity. Also pay attention to how it may begin to shape your interactions with your circumstances and with others.

3. "Nothing can separate me from the love of God; there is no condemnation for those who are in Christ. Amen."

Take a few moments to sit in, soak in, and savor the unchangeable-ever-lasting-nothing-can-separate-you-from-it love that God has poured out into you (Rom. 5:5).

Prayer of
Awareness

This prayer helps you to be aware of the ongoing invitations and challenges from God that are communicated and revealed by the ongoing circumstances of your life.

The prayer flows from Psalm 139:23–24:

> *Search me, O God, and know my heart! Try me and know my thoughts.*
> *And see if there be any grievous ["hurtful" (NASB); "wicked" (KJV)]*
> *way in me, and lead me in the way everlasting!*

When this prayer is faithfully practiced, it transforms you into a person who:

a. knows God as one who loves you, is with you, and one who comes to experience yourself as the beloved of God.

b. senses and welcomes the convicting role of the Spirit so that you can turn from your sin (hurtful, wicked ways), embrace life, and learn that there is no condemnation in Christ.

c. develops an awareness of the inner movements of your spirit toward God or away from God, as well as recognizes the voice of Jesus—the Good Shepherd who calls you by name and leads you. You become a discerning person.

d. becomes aware of and admits the wrong choices you have made, choices that led to death not life, and—once you've admitted them—experiences God's forgiveness, grace, and love.

e. acknowledges and owns your inability to live this life by your own power and affirms your ongoing need for the empowering of Jesus in your daily life.

The five steps of this prayer will be explained below.

Step 1. Being Grateful (silence and gratitude): The Bible reminds us that every good thing comes from heaven above (James 1:17), and this step invites you to recall to mind and heart the *particular* good things you have experienced since your last Prayer of Awareness, good things that testify to the love, goodness, and care of God in your life. This step helps you to see God's grace in your life even during the tough times and, when practiced over time, fosters a growing trust in and love for God and a deeper awareness of God's love for you. (And recent studies have shown that cultivating such an inner posture of gratitude can increase happiness levels.)

Step 2. Being Open (searching): The purpose of this step is to sensitize you to the convicting work of the Spirit and prompt you to respond accordingly—turning away from hurtful ways and turning toward God, thus being free to more fully live into and out of who God created you to be.

There are four things to know regarding Step 2:

    a.   You ask God to show you your hurtful ways—you are not to do this by reviewing your day (Ps. 139:23–24). *Often God will not show you anything at this step.* Rather, this step is expressing the desire of your heart to know your sin, so that as you walk through your day the Holy Spirit will reveal your hurtful way in the moment.

    b.   When God does choose to reveal your sin, it is important to remember that this God-given awareness is a gift that leads to freedom, confirms your status as a child of God, and is an answer to your prayers.

    c.   God tends to reveal one area at a time. If it seems like God is revealing multiple areas, seek to discover the underlying theme that links the seemingly divergent areas.

    d.   This step is not about condemnation, for there is no condemnation in Christ (Rom. 8:1). If you feel the weight that condemnation brings, this is not from God and it is a false guilt that leads to destruction and death. The true guilt (revelation) mentioned above brings freedom and awareness of God's love and involvement in your life.

False Guilt and Step 2

"Just because we feel guilty does not mean the Spirit of God is convicting our hearts regarding sin. And the key test or indicator in this regard is any feelings of condemnation. False guilt is burdensome. False guilt condemns us. True guilt—that which is the fruit of the Spirit's ministry—is liberating; it leads to freedom... It may well be that most of the times we feel guilty the guilt is not from God. Therefore the matter of the *convicting ministry of the Spirit demands discernment (emphasis mine)*." –Gordon T. Smith[1]

Step 3. Being Aware (review and awareness): In this step, you look back over the time between this and your previous prayer of awareness, asking yourself, "Where have the interactions and circumstances of my life been taking me; to God (volitional consolation) or away from God (volitional desolation)?"

This step is not solely concerned with the *what* of your emotions; rather the focus is on *where* your emotions are taking you—to God or somewhere else.

This step helps you to notice the inner movements of your heart. This awareness gives you the opportunity to adjust as needed, as well as the opportunity to name and *explore any resistance*, and/or the whys behind those things that took you away from God.

Step 3 also allows you to review your day, looking for the invitations and/or challenges that God presented to you, and then exploring the what and why of your interplay with God during these times. Did you say yes to God? Were you unaware until now of any such encounters? Did you resist the invitation and/or challenges of God, or even refuse to follow the voice of the Good Shepherd? It is in and through the regular practice of this step that you gradually become a discerning person—sensitive and aware of the subtle movements of the Spirit and able to discern the voice of Jesus amidst the constant clamor of your daily life. Becoming aware is the pathway to discernment.

Step 4. Being Forgiven/Loved (talking with Jesus): In step 4 you hear the earth-shattering roar of God, but not a roar of displeasure or condemnation. If you listen carefully from the deep places of your heart, you will hear that it is a high-spirited cry announcing God's love for you, God's grace extended to you, and God's everlasting forgiveness spoken to you.

In this step, you ask God's forgiveness for anything that came up in Steps 2 or 3—anything that needs forgiveness or acknowledgement. Once again as in Step 2, this is not about condemnation but about being released from guilt and replacing it with the experience of God's grace and unconditional love.

- Name the Wrong(s) – confess your sin of commission or omission.
- Own Responsibility – own your role regarding your sin of commission or omission.
- Accept Forgiveness – Soak in God's love, grace and forgiveness.

Step 5. Being Connected (abiding): In this step, you simply acknowledge that you cannot live a God-honoring life alone, but you need God's abiding presence (John 15:5) and an ever-deepening internalization of God's love for you (Eph. 3:17–19), faithfulness to you (Heb. 13:5), and power within you (Eph. 3:16).

This prayer practice is transforming, for it enables you to choose wisely throughout a day and a lifetime. It teaches you to discern the movements of your heart (toward God or away from God—Step 3); it fosters a sensitivity to the Spirit (Steps 2 and 3) and reminds you that you cannot do it alone (Step 5). It is built on a foundation of knowing that God is with you, for you, predisposed to shower you with love and grace (Steps 1 and 4) and to fill you with power to live in a way that honors and glorifies God—by freeing you to live as God created you to be (Step 5).

15 Keys to
God-Honoring Decisions

I know many are desirous of a list to live by, so I am providing the keys below, not as steps to work through one by one, but as tenets of discernment lived into over time. Christian discernment is a way of life—a life open and yielded to God, dependent on the Spirit, indifferent to all but God's will, demonstrating a Spirit-infused-spontaneous-incisiveness. The God-honoring life of discernment is marked by an ability to live freely and lightly, embracing the unforced rhythm of God's grace and reliant on God's amazing love.

1. God is involved in your life and committed to leading and guiding you through it. Soak, swim, wade, float in God's love—God loves you, likes you and loves loving you!

2. Let your internalization of God's amazing love for you—you are the beloved of God—cultivate a growing love for God and trust in God.

3. Become indifferent to all else but God's will being done on earth as it is in heaven.

4. Grow in awareness of yourself, your heart, your surroundings, the Spirit, and the ways God communicates to you in expected and unexpected places.

5. Grow in humility and dependency, acknowledging your need for God, for Jesus, for their wisdom, guidance, and the leading of the Holy Spirit.

6. Learn to listen, discern, and follow the inner promptings of the Spirit, so that you are able to hear the whisper of God and sense the drop of water hitting a rock or gently landing on a sponge.

7. Learn to engage with scripture as a place of encounter with God and transformation into Christlikeness.

8. Let go of enslavement to reason, the need to do what makes sense, and embrace the mathematics of faith (2 fish + 5 loaves of bread + **Jesus** = a catered meal for 5,000 people). The heart has reasons that reason does not know.

9. Allow time to make a decision. *Do not force* yourself to make a decision or to rush into a decision (be drawn, not driven).

10. Resist the temptation to make elaborate plans.

11. Learn to trust God and the process.

12. Do NOT change a decision you made in a time of consolation during a time of desolation.

13. There are two types of decisions: changeable and unchangeable. The changeable decision God leads you to make today, God may very well lead you to change tomorrow.

14. Keep discerning. Christian discernment is a way of life.

15. Never forget your four aces of decision-making.

This book was written to help you order your life in such a way that these 15 keys will not be exercises you do, but will become the very essence of how you live.

WEBSITE
INFORMATION

On the home page of b-ing.org, you will find a tab dedicated to this book: "Christian Discernment". A section under that tab contains materials for use in a small group setting. The first few pages present tips that can help a small group be a place of safety and sharing, therefore creating a place of transformation. You will also find brief videos that correspond to each chapter, reflection questions, and exercises to do as a group, and even some prayer prompts.

END NOTES

Chapter One: The What and Why of Discernment?

1. Calvin, John. *Institutes of the Christian Religion*, ed. John T. McNeill, trans. Ford Lewis Battles (Louisville: Westminster John Knox Press, 1960 [1559]), p. 35 (*Inst.* 1.1.1).

Chapter Three: Whose Are You?

1. A. W. Tozer, *The Knowledge of the Holy* (New York: Harper & Row, 1961), p. 9.

2. A.W. Tozer, *The Knowledge of the Holy* (New York: Harper & Row, 1961), p. 10.

3. Julian of Norwich, *Julian of Norwich Showings* (Mahwah: Paulist Press, 1978), p. 130.

4. Gordon T. Smith, *Voice of Jesus: Discernment, Prayer and the Witness of the Spirit* (Downers Grove: 2003), p. 74, 78-79

Chapter Four: Who Are You?

1. Brennan Manning, *Abba's Child: The Cry of the Heart for Intimate Belonging* (Colorado Springs: NAVPRESS 2015), p. 42.

Chapter Five: Be Free

1. Anthony De Mello, *The Way of the Heart* (New York: Double Day, 1995), p. 28.

2. Anthony De Mello, *The Way of the Heart* (New York: Double Day, 1995), p. 113-114.

Chapter Six: Be Aware

1. Elizabeth Barrett Browning, *Aurora Leigh* (Oxford: Oxford University Press, 2008), p. 246.

2. Jean-Pierre de Caussade, *Abandonment to Divine Providence* (New York: Double Day, 1975).

3. Dallas Willard, *The Spirit of the Disciplines* (San Francisco: Harper Collins, 1991), p. 101.

4. Thomas Merton, *New Seeds of Contemplation* (New York: New Directions Publishing, 1973), p. 84.

5. Marjorie J. Thompson, *Soul Feast: An Invitation to the Christian Life* (Louisville: Westminster John Knox Press), p. 36.

6. Margaret Silf, *Inner Compass: An Invitation to Ignatian Spirituality* (Chicago: Loyola Press, 1998), p. 52-53.

Chapter Seven: God's Will

1. Dallas Willard, In Search of Divine Guidance: Developing a Conversational Relationship with God (San Francisco: Zondervan, 1993), p. 107.

2. Garry Freisen, *Decision Making and the Will of God* (Portland: Multnomah Press, 1980), p. 35.

Chapter Eight: The Role of the Holy Spirit

1. Richard F. Lovelace. *Dynamics of Spiritual Life* (Downers Grove: InterVarsity, 1979), p. 131.

Chapter Nine: The Role of Scripture

1. Richard Foster, Celebration of Discipline (San Francisco: Harper and Row, 1978), p. 56.

2. Gordon T. Smith, *Voice of Jesus: Discernment, Prayer and the Witness of the Spirit* (Downers Grove: InterVarsity, 2003), p. 31.

3. J. I. Packer, *Knowing God* (Downers Grove: InterVarsity, 1973), p. 23.

4. Bruce Demarest, *Satisfy Your Soul* (Colorado Springs: NavPress, 1999), p. 133.

Chapter Eleven: Christian Discernment: What does look like?

1. Dallas Willard, In Search of Divine Guidance: Developing a Conversational Relationship with God (San Francisco: Zondervan, 1993), p. 101-102.

2. Bob Mumford, *Take Another Look at Guidance* (Raleigh: Lifechangers Publishing, 1999), p. 172.

Chapter Twelve: Discernment of Spirits

1. Dean Brackley, The Call of Discernment in Troubled Times: New Prospectives on the Transformative Wisdom of Ignatius of Loyola (New York: Crossroad Publishing, 2004), p. 137.

Chapter Thirteen: Decision-making: Pros and Cons

1. Thomas Green, *Weeds Among the Wheat* (Notre Dame: Ave Maria Press, 2000), p. 88.

Chapter Sixteen: Adult Faith

1. Garry Freisen, *Decision Making and the Will of God* (Portland: Multnomah Press, 1980), p. 246.

Chapter Nineteen: Desire and Motivation

1. C.S. Lewis, *The Weight of Glory and Other Addresses* (Grand Rapids: Eerdmans, 1965), p. 1-2.

2. John Burnaby, *Amor Dei: A Study of the Religion of St. Augustine* (London: Hodder & Stoughton, 1938), 97, quoting *In Ep. Jo. Tr.* 4. 6.

3. Thomas Merton, *Thoughts in Solitude* (Boston: Shambhala, 1958), p. 55.

4. Wilkie Au, The Discerning Heart: Exploring the Christian Path (Mahwah: Paulist Press, 2006), p. 145

5. Robert Jonas, as quoted in *Discernment Reading the Signs in Daily Life,* by Henri J. Nouwen with Michael J. Christensen and Rebecca Laird (New York: Harper Collins, 2013) p. 176.

Chapter Twenty: Heart and Head

1. Oswald Chambers, *My Utmost for His Highest* (New York: Dodd, Mead and Company, 1935), p. 222.

2. Gordon T. Smith, *Voice of Jesus: Discernment, Prayer and the Witness of the Spirit* (Downers Grove: InterVarsity, 2003), p. 65.

3. David Benner, Surrender to Love: Discovering the Heart of Christian Spirituality (Downers Grove: InterVarsity, 2003), p. 31.

3. Blaise Pascal, *Pensées and Other Writings*, trans. Honor Levi (New York: Oxford University Press, 1995), p.158.

Appendix: Prayer of Awareness

1. Gordon T. Smith, *Voice of Jesus: Discernment, Prayer and the Witness of the Spirit* (Downers Grove: 2003), p. 93.

ABOUT THE AUTHOR

Larry Warner, who refers to himself as the beloved of God and enjoys going barefoot, is a teacher, a pastor and a spiritual director. He is an associate professor in the area of spiritual formation, Ignatian spirituality, and spiritual direction, currently teaching at the Institute of Spiritual Formation at Biola University and Bethel Seminary, San Diego, and has taught in the Master of Ministry program, Pt. Loma Nazarene University.

As a spiritual director, Larry meets with pastors and church leadership throughout the world. He is a retreat leader, author of *Journey with Jesus* and co-author of *Imaginative Prayer for Youth Ministry*. In 2005 he founded b (b-ing.org), a spiritual support organization for pastors, missionaries, seminarians and church staffs, which encourages them to open to God's love and to live Jesus in new and deeper ways.

Larry has a varied vocational background. He was a youth pastor for eleven years, a Los Angeles Deputy Sheriff for six years, and a senior pastor for ten years before founding and leading b for nearly twelve years. Though roles and experiences changed, his passion has remained the same: to help people more fully embrace God's love and to live more fully into and out of the person God has called and created them to be, free to love and serve others in life giving ways.

Larry has been married for over 37 years; he is a father of four and a grandfather of four.

ACKNOWLEDGEMENTS

There are many who gave me valuable input and provided timely encouragement as I was writing this book.

My wife, Donna, was a constant support, even when I went away for long blocks of time to write. She was and is a wonderful partner —an encourager and at times a needed prodder who helped to keep me moving forward to completion.

Additionally, Erin, Diane, Ben, Stephen, Steve, and Christine each took time to read portions of the book providing valuable suggestions, insights, and encouraging comments.

My editor, Jessica Snell, was invaluable. She offered excellent suggestions, asked great questions, gently challenged me on pieces of theology, grammar, the use of certain phrases and particular pronouns, and provided encouraging words as well. The time, energy, and expertise she expended on this project took it to a whole new level, helping to bring greater value to the reader. My interactions with Jessica and her partnering with me on this journey were an unexpected gift from God.

Christine Smith, a former student and a talented and exceedingly creative person who designed my cover, was a joy to work with. She extended me grace and demonstrated patience as we moved ever closer to the final cover. She is a great mix of artist and writer.

And finally there was one person who was HUGELY instrumental in helping to get this project from the *God's-told-me-to-write-this* stage to the *it-is-finished-you-are-holding-it-in-your-hands* completion. That person was Gail Steel. Gail was a constant encouragement and support all along the way.

She took my ROUGH first drafts and helped to make sense of my words and turn convoluted sentences and paragraphs into something intelligible—offering suggestions, deleting, re-working large portions of material, and also providing timely encouragement.

As I look back through my life, it seems God always raises up a key person at just the right time to help me move into God's current invitation; for this project that person was Gail. We began the journey as co-laborers and ended the journey as dear friends—another gift from God along the way.

Made in the USA
San Bernardino, CA
22 February 2018